T0283271

Advance Praise for
My Disappearing Mother

"A searing, breathtaking memoir many have needed for so long. Finnamore clearly shares literary DNA with Joan Didion and Kurt Vonnegut, yet hers is an entirely unique voice. A memoir, yes, but this is also an essential map and guidebook for the country of Dementia that possesses a near universal appeal. As your heart breaks, your spirit will soar."

—Augusten Burroughs, #1 *New York Times* bestselling author

"There is Finnamore's brave and open heart; her eye for what gleams in the rubble; her generosity, humor, confusion, and grief; but grace shines on everything. She is also a brilliant writer. I can't wait to get my hands on this book."

—Abigail Thomas, *New York Times* bestselling author of *What Comes Next and How To Like It*

"Suzanne's memoir about her mother in Dementia is beautiful and consoling and deeply felt, full of both joy and sorrow, and also, not for nothing, gorgeously written. I was stopped in my tracks. It is an astonishing book."

—Elizabeth McCracken, bestselling author of *The Souvenir Museum* and winner of the PEN/New England Award

"This elegant memoir does the impossible: it makes the tragic beautiful. It also offers a service: providing solace to those whose mothers have dementia, showing how best to deal with what we cannot prevent. Luminous, gripping, and unexpectedly funny, Finnamore pays homage to a remarkable life, but she does much more than that. In teaching us how she looks at her own declining mother—with understanding, love, and happiness—Finnamore is, in effect, teaching us how to see."

—Darin Strauss, *New York Times* bestselling author of *Half a Life* and winner of a National Book Critics Circle Award

"*My Disappearing Mother: A Memoir of Magic and Loss in the Country of Dementia* is a truly stunning piece of writing by Suzanne Finnamore. The magic is real."

—Julie Klam, *New York Times* bestselling author of *The Almost Legendary Morris Sisters*

My
Disappearing
Mother

My Disappearing Mother

A Memoir of Magic and Loss in the Country of Dementia

Suzanne Finnamore

Post Hill
PRESS

A POST HILL PRESS BOOK
ISBN: 979-8-88845-015-4
ISBN (eBook): 979-8-88845-016-1

My Disappearing Mother:
A Memoir of Magic and Loss in the Country of Dementia
© 2023 by Suzanne Finnamore
All Rights Reserved

Post Hill Press
New York • Nashville
posthillpress.com

Published in the United States of America
1 2 3 4 5 6 7 8 9 10

To all the daughters, sons, friends and spouses left behind.

"One must say Yes to life and embrace it whenever it is found—and it is found in terrible places; nevertheless, there it is.

"For nothing is fixed, forever and forever and forever, it is not fixed; the earth is always shifting, the light is always changing, the sea does not cease to grind down rock. Generations do not cease to be born, and we are responsible to them because we are the only witnesses they have.

"The sea rises, the light fails, lovers cling to each other, and children cling to us. The moment we cease to hold each other, the moment we break faith with one another, the sea engulfs us and the light goes out."

~*James Baldwin*

CONTENTS

PREFACE

Six years ago, my husband and I moved two thousand miles to be near my stepfather and my mother, Bunny, who is now entering the seventh stage of dementia. There is no eighth stage.

As the months passed, I began to think of Dementia as a real place, where beloved and ancient queens and kings retire. A place where linear time doesn't exist and the rules of society are laid aside. Whenever I go to my parent's double-wide mobile home in Hayward, California, I am really traveling to Dementia. Seen this way, I allow for magic to happen and for there to be a boundary between myself and the slippery slope of despair. I acknowledge another world, about which I know nothing. I assume nothing other than her presence in a different land and her agency within its boundaries. Each time I go, it's different. I've learned to set expectations aside, like an umbrella on a sunny day.

There are precious few conversations about Dementia, even though many of us will cross its borders. There is stigma; there is shame. There is great fear; there is cultural taboo. We turn our back on it and pretend it isn't there…an outland which the healthy feel entitled to shun. We avoid; we minimize; we catastrophize. We make jokes, whistling past the graveyard. Most families, like mine, have not the funds for a memory facility. We build our own, and we fashion a makeshift waystation out of devotion.

It can be harrowing. It can be surreal. A replica planet hovering above our own, mysterious, unfathomable. A quixotic land, full of resurrection and common miracles. Monsters and hallucinations live there; loss gallops through its streets. But where my mother goes, I go.

As a coping mechanism, I began an inventory of observations. I picked up stray gems I came across in the ruins—the smaller, the better. I began to actively search for mortality insights, the gifts we are meant to find, our reward for not turning away. As I helped my stepfather clear their house of excess, I found unexpected clues to my mother's past, to my ancestors in Puerto Rico. A fossil record of the Boricua who made me.

Like all who travel, I was enriched.

Years slipped by. I watched my mother dramatically decline. I grew despondent. I looked for things to read, from a grieving son or daughter like myself. There weren't enough. *Still Alice* is lovely, but it's a novel. Elizabeth Berg wrote a brilliant memoir about her parents, as did Patti Davis. I wanted more, a roomful. As many books as there are about murder and true crime, perhaps. Dementia is a true crime, I feel. There are fifty-five million people suffering from it right now. Another ten million a year will come. It deeply impacts families, financially and emotionally. The needs of caregivers are massive; the isolation is crippling. I am virtually my seventy-eight-year-old stepfather's only confidante, save one or two surviving friends. There are thousands of militias out there, waging the same battle of love and duty, a courage brigade deployed by a random occurrence. The grown children, the spouses, the friends. The people surrounding the voiceless and the marginalized.

A book, I thought, might be company for those tethered to their homes. It might be a tiny lifeline, a friend who understands this murky country. Many of my closest friends are books. They never sicken or die. They ask nothing when I have nothing to give.

In 2021, on the advice of my grief therapist, I began posting tiny excerpts on social media about my mother's life and her time in Dementia. I wanted to speak on it, a broader conversation. Not just about dementia but about the rich and gorgeous generation it attempts to rub out. Almost at once, I received private messages. Distant friends I hadn't heard from in years. Also, strangers, who instantly became something more. People like me. They needed more, they said. *Keep going*, they said. They wanted, it seemed, what I want.

I want a book that honors my Boricua ancestors and my mother's life. I want a book that acknowledges that dementia isn't the defining chapter of a life; that it goes on in the midst of life, which also goes on. I want a book that attests to the fact that in a world full of disease, there is an abiding and supernatural force of love. That because of this, the sadness and the horror can be borne. That laughter can live alongside grief. That it must.

I want a book offering verbatim tools my grief therapist taught me, for the process of caretaking and grieving the living, the people we love who are dying slowly in front of our eyes. I want a book to hand folks who find themselves on marathons of loss, and I want to offer them humor as well as clues. I want a book that is a sign in the desert and a series of water stands with balloons. I want a travel guide for the daughters and sons and spouses of Dementia. I want them to not walk alone as I have. I want a book that celebrates my mother and all women born in poverty who climb out against brutal odds, women who are in fact at the highest risk for dementia.

I want a book that is a testament to ordinary enchantment. How even the harshest landscape has hidden alchemy, treasures waiting to be mined at its lowest regions.

And so, although no one has asked, or because no one has asked, it seems my job to report back.

Few speak on Dementia. But I will.

To travel in a foreign land, you need a map. It can be an incomplete map; it probably will be. It can be a flawed map. This one certainly is. Nonetheless, it's a starting point, a guide. A way in and, just possibly, a way out.

Dementia is the most foreign country I know, the least charted. I send love to those who travel there.

ONE

What Was Lost

"Now and then, though, someone does begin to grow differently. Instead of down, his feet grow up toward the sky. But we do our best to discourage awkward things like that.

"'What happens to them?' insisted Milo.

"'Oddly enough, they often grow ten times the size of everyone else,' said Alec thoughtfully, 'and I've heard that they walk among the stars.'"

—Norton Juster, *The Phantom Tollbooth*

Incantation, 2017

If I stand in front of her, I am myself. If I leave the room, I become a malevolent intruder. There's a revolving door in my mother's brain I pass through again and again.

Today, I process decades, cleaning and organizing and recycling and donating, offloading her entire life to strangers. I create the illusion of order in a house where reality has no set meaning. If this isn't childhood, I don't know what is.

I position myself in her sight line. Say the incantation, in the correct timbre.

Mommy.

Her face opens.

She has forgotten how to walk. She has refused to try since she fell last year.

A broken leg, the hospital said.

She was discharged. But both legs were broken. They somehow missed the other fracture, the billowing, black bruise. And so, we brought her back. Her life expectancy in a nursing home would have been eight months.

In this, her adopted land, the poor and the brown are discarded like coffee grinds.

But this is what we are for. We pick her back up. Clean her. Reenthrone her.

The Last Reading

It's July 2009, and For Sale signs dot our hill like pock marks; we've had one outside our house for months. I've lost my job in advertising, barely managing to sell my house, the bank eating whatever profit existed. My nine-year-old son Pablo and I are leaving California for North Carolina. We're staying at my parents' double-wide mobile home with our two cats, Potatoes and Vixen. We are leaving the next day. We are afraid, but we are leaving.

In my mother's office where she tells fortunes is an embroidered fringed brocade skirt over a small circular wooden table. On it, her tarot cards are wrapped in a silk scarf. She wants to give me a reading before I leave.

"Sit with both feet on the floor," she says, drawing her Hawaiian muumuu around her short bulk as she settles into her glider chair. Her tight black perm makes a halo around her head, her nails are unvarnished. A crystal on a leather cord hangs from her neck, along with a plastic red heart. Her feet are bare. This is my favorite moment. The sloughing of what was brought into the room.

We breathe together. Her eyes are closed; her hands are clasped. I can see her feeling the room with her mind. A variety of clocks tick all around us. When she opens her eyes, the reading begins. She is no longer my mother; she is something else.

She unwraps the cards and begins to shuffle, her hands moving steadily, automatically. She shuffles cards and looks above my head and to the right, with the air of someone emptying themselves. She stops.

"Mira," she says, pointing to the deck on the table with one bent finger. *Here.*

I touch the deck, my finger a wand.

She gathers it up and cuts the cards. She lays the cards out in a row, face down. Just three cards. I am not getting the full ten card treatment. That's for clients. That's for outsiders.

"This is the past," she says, flipping the first card.

Temperance. There is Archangel Michael. A tall figure in silver robes, hands at his side, palms turned out.

"You held things together. You kept things balanced."

"You were a good wife," she says, as if realizing this for the first time. She points to the card.

"But see how he has one foot in the river and one on the land? Half conscious, half unconscious. So you go through life, a saint watching over you, but limited. Half asleep."

My mother makes these leaps, and I can but follow.

She turns over the middle card.

"This is Now."

Three of Cups, reversed. Three figures that dance with cups raised in a circle.

I dislike the reversed cards—drawing them feels like failing at a crucial test. But anything upright would have seemed false. A lie. My mother doesn't lie.

"You are on your head. That's you and Pablo and me…no, someone else."

I feel flat. I want to go to sleep.

"Your cups were emptied, all three of you. Your wine turned to ashes. Pleasure turned to pain."

The urge to sleep grows. I speak with effort.

"I feel like that should be the Death card," I say, morose.

"The Death card is a beautiful card. It means change and transformation. You should be so lucky as to get the Death card," she says tartly.

She points to the Three of Cups again. The figures dance gaily, holding hands and raising a single gold chalice between them.

"But see them as the three Graces, see them clearly. They are still with you, right now. And they can flip at any time and become upright." She turns the card upright for me, to demonstrate. She leaves it that way. A mini spell.

"This is the future," she says, flipping the last card.

Three of Wands. A man holds a globe and looks out to sea. He holds one tall wand, and two others are behind him, unnoticed.

"He is looking out and waiting. You're waiting. The ships you had are out to sea."

Out to sea is such a comforting way to think of a failed marriage and job loss, I think. Something that is gone but in the world still.

"But look. The three wands are still in his possession, and they flower. But he doesn't know that. He keeps looking at what he has lost."

It's almost as though I can hear the waves, feel the hopeless wind.

"The magic is still yours," my mother says. "You will wait. You will have faith."

I start to cry. What is faith, I think. What is it?

Bunny has mercy on me and pulls a fourth, wild bonus card:

The Chariot: a golden, celestial cart drawn by two sphinxes, driven by a Knight.

"You are on your path," she says. "There is no danger. This Knight is with you, and he drives you there."

"What knight? I'm no damsel. Look at me."

I am wearing mismatched pajamas and a bandana on my head. On my feet are Yeti slippers.

My mother shakes her head.

"I have no idea."

A tall dark stranger? Is she serious?

"You're just telling me what I want to hear," I say.

"No," she says. "I'm not."

She opens her eyes. Places her hands on her hips. Stands up, reaching for her cane with a sigh. Another one in the books.

"He may be strange, but he is coming to your aid, and not with small force," Bunny says.

When we landed in Durham, North Carolina, I was fifty. What my mother use to call *Five-Oh*.

Don't get old, mija, she'd say, examining her face in a lighted mirror, tweezing her eyebrows with a clown's open expression of amazement.

I bought a tiny house, sight unseen—based on pictures on the internet. Eight hundred square feet. We knew no one. A neighbor brought us a peach pie, redolent with cinnamon and swathed in tin foil.

An email arrives. Only twenty dollars for a month of online dating. I look in the mirror, smooth my hair back from my forehead. I buy a box of Clairol Root Touch-Up.

Every day they send me a Daily Five Picks. I see a man with silver hair. Tom, forty-nine, Chapel Hill. Two children. Divorced. I look at his profile. He looks at mine. We go out for dinner, a place called Revolution. He never leaves.

Thirteen years ago today.

What if I hadn't opened the email? What if he hadn't?

Everything rests on the fulcrum of this moment. Fate waits to pivot. Love waits for its lever, to fly into a life and wreck it forever. To save it.

She Came Across the Ocean

She was born Olga Iris Irizarry during the height of the Depression to Leonor and Felipe in Mayaguez. At two, she was ferried to New York by Felipe's mother, Abuelita Rufina, who gave her to her childless daughter, Sarah. Felipe had no use for her. Leonor had no use for her. She was passed around like a bottle. Inside the bottle, a skeleton key. She would fit where she was.

She remembers being lifted to the portholes and looking out, taking in the good smell of the ocean. The steamship

Borinquen took her and other Boricuas from Puerto Rico. Fear was not present.

Motherless she came, sailing the steamship from one island to another, her baby legs bowed with rickets. A thousand lice eggs nestled in her black hair. Worms crawled from her nose and mouth, looking for a way out. A home.

To this moment she came, bedridden now, able to travel only in her mind, full of holes but with pockets of memory still. She gets to keep the early ones, the good ones. God has done what he could and is tired.

New York saved her. She would have many lives; this was the second. Sarah and her husband Ferdinand Nunez adopted her, naming her Bunny. She spent a month in Lennox Hill before springing forth like Lazarus to her new life in Manhattan.

She troubles herself less and less with anything real now. She is ascending and descending at once. Dementia has no set gravity.

But when I come, she surfaces from where she is. She gathers herself like a synchronized swimmer, with what I know is a great effort, and glides to me from the depth. She says three words, ones she knew then. I say them back.

In Mayaguez 1937, another baby came to Leonor. My mother's brother. He died of starvation. He has no name.

They are alive now, as I tell their story. The ghosts of Leonor and her second child rise, hearing their names, or the place where a name should be. They come into my bedroom, sit close. Listen.

Boricua, a Definition

Boricua are people born in Puerto Rico. Borinquen was the island's name before the conquering Europeans in big ships christened it Puerto Rico. They thought to obliterate, but Taino blood is strong. A small bit is enough.

In San Juan, I saw people on the streets who looked like me. I blended and felt fully at home, exalted. A plain sword placed back in its richly jeweled scabbard.

When the European ships first appeared on the horizon, the Taino were unable to see them. It was not a form they recognized. They thought they were waves, clouds, or a monstrous turtle on the sea. An apparition of the gods. Some saw nothing at all, until all was made clear. The demons had come.

I was born in California, but my blood is Taino. A fact I never forget, especially now.

The indigenous people of the Caribbean believed in the existence of life after death. They practiced burying tribe members with their belongings, placing food and water next to the casket to accompany them onto their next life.

For Bunny, I will place a box of Ding Dongs. Her Christmas tree earrings that she wore throughout December and well into January. Her favorite Hawaiian muumuu, with tropical birds. A bowl of rice and milk, her comfort food. Books. A pair of red shoes for when she can dance again.

Parade of Faces

Bunny convalesces and speaks her litany of adoration, prompted by the extensive and ongoing family photo slideshow that Ron made to keep her brain engaged and entertained, and to spark conversation for those who don't know what to say when they visit Bunny. Every waking hour when she and Ron are not watching something else, her loved ones splash across the giant flatscreen television in front of her, what we call *The Parade of Faces*.

"I love Abuelita so much."

A picture of my great grandmother, looking majestic in a lawn chair in the front yard of her housing project, surrounded by flowers and birthday gifts from her six children. Her blue eyes laser at me.

"She loves you too!"

"I love Daddy so much."

A picture of Ferdinand in his soldier's uniform. Black hair, thin moustache.

"He loves you too!"

"Look, there's your grandson!"

"Cute!"

"There's Uncle Pinkie!" I say. Her half-brother Philip, born to the family that Felipe created to wash his mouth of her and Leonor.

It's an old script, but I put everything I have into it, and soon I find that I am right there with my mother. I am marveling at each photo as it appears in front of her bed, marveling as if we are at the Tonys, and we have just sighted Rita Moreno.

Today Ron has gone to Costco and to the bank. She grows more tense as the minutes progress, as do I.

"I hope Dick comes home soon," she says, placing my father's name where Ron's should be.

"Dad's dead, Mom. He's already home," I say.

"How long was I married to him?" she asks, unfazed.

"Fourteen years."

We add up the years she was married to Dick and to Ron. Sixty-four years. My mother was single for six months in the sixties. An orphan's decision made long ago.

"When is Daddy coming back?" she says. Worried.

"Soon, Mommy!"

Today Ron is a stranger, is her father Ferdinand, is her ex-husband. He has a revolving door all his own.

Daily she grows more worn out, thinner and more stretched, like Frodo after carrying the ring for too long.

Now the surface is showing. The original die.

What It Is

Not a disease but a group of syndromes. Too clever to be one, it slips inside the many. It creeps along slowly and silently, one brain cell at a time, showing itself and then hiding again, a game of *Mother May I* played with a monster. It preys on the elderly and infirm. A purse snatcher, a rapist. You won't recognize it. You won't see it coming until it is well advanced.

They are looking for a cure. Looking, it seems to me, not very hard. Counting on attrition. Watching the bottom line. It will come for them, too.

It may or may not be hereditary. You can't catch it from a kiss or the air. It chooses you.

Diaphanous, blinding, impossible to pin down. A mustard gas, it hobbles. It eats reason like a marvelous big buffet and then as an encore, it takes the body. It dashes intellect like a light, then reaches for hope itself to quash.

What cure can be found for evil?

The Sorceress

At eighteen, Bunny was in the newspaper for typing a hundred words a minute on a manual typewriter. Before she gave birth to my brother and me, she sang and danced for enlisted soldiers in Pasadena. In 1953, she dropped out of college to marry my father and have children. She was now Bunny Finnamore: her third name, her third life. In 1967, when he left for higher ground in San Francisco, she put on kitten heels and went to Goodwill to buy clothes. She got a secretarial job, where she met and married the love of her life, my stepfather Ron. She became what she needed to be.

Now she was Bunny Mathews. Life number four.

A voracious reader, her walls were lined with books, from Homer to James Baldwin to Jacqueline Susann and Colette. She was a scholar of metaphysics and spoke in wonder of Edgar Cayce and Krishnamurti and the Persian mystics. She took up the study of tarot and *I Ching*. She was Sarah's child and had grown up devout Nazarene. Yet she was also a child of Leonor, from the land of Santeria, where herb lore and portents were commonplace, part of island culture. Blood sang to blood.

She gave me hundreds of readings, often strikingly prescient, delivered with her breezy conversational style. She saw my youth in perfect array when I saw it as a jumble of folly. She'd lay out ten cards in a Celtic cross, and my life would unfold in front of our hands. Phone conversations could also morph into a reading: I was going to change jobs; I was going to be betrayed by a friend. "…but just smile and send her love. She doesn't know any better, *tonta*." *Little fool.*

When I cried over a man who jilted me for another, she offered no bromides. I should get a cat, and I should name it

11

Clive, she instructed. I went to buy milk and saw a kitten in a box marked FREE. Clive was a Maine Coon with pointy fur-tufted ears I'd whisper into. A large cat, a cat like a person, who laid on my chest when I was poorly, arms and legs outstretched. My mother said the man would marry the woman but would be back in twenty years, when it was too late. This transpired.

In 1980, she quit her secretarial job and became a professional clairvoyant, working out of the enclosed front porch room of their mobile home, and giving workshops on tarot. Her professional name was Adrian—her fifth name, her fifth life. How many lives can one woman have? My mother set no arbitrary limits. Adrian was booked months in advance, with devoted clients coming from as far as Los Angeles. One hour for seventy-five dollars, including a cassette tape recording. She said she didn't really need the cards, but her clients did.

If I just start talking, she told me, *they'll think I'm nuts.*

In My Mother's House

In my mother's houses live a variety of talking clocks. A bird-call clock, where twelve o'clock is a great horned owl. A clock with talking Looney Tunes characters, Bugs Bunny, Yosemite Sam, Road Runner, Speedy Gonzales, Pepe Le Pew, Daffy Duck, Marvin the Martian, Tweety, Tasmanian Devil, Foghorn, Sylvester the Cat. So that Porky Pig will announce,

"It's uh th-thr-thr-three o'clock. I think."

"Eeet iz five, mon petit…" says Pepe Le Pew at exactly 5:15.

None of the clocks are on time, which adds to the magic. You choose what time it is for you personally. You go by that. There are sensors on the clocks, so that when it's dark, the characters don't talk. During the day, it is riotous. A Mad Hatter's house, a tea party always in session.

In my mother's house, everything was always in its place. When I entered, she would hang up my coat and purse at once. I hugged things close to my body so as not to be organized away to one of her many cupboards of useful items, carefully lined with flowered Contact paper. In her medicine cabinet, Vicks VapoRub reigned and was used to cure everything: colds, the flu, sore muscles, menstrual cramps, headaches, fever. The aroma of mysterious healing wafted from the blue jar. I have a jar I smell just to travel back to this time.

In my mother's house, no one was allowed to feel sorry for themselves, and everyone was loved, or else they were not allowed in my mother's house, a bastion of safety. Those in need, went there. She had many friends and admirers. All gone now.

In the land of linear time, this is the survivor tax. But where she wanders, all are reborn.

Detective Bunny

When she was fifty, my mother began a quest to find her birth mother, Leonor. She knew her name was now Garcia and that she had more children with her husband. Her siblings, in Puerto Rico. She would never find them.

Her adopted mother Sarah rarely spoke of Leonor, as though to do so would invoke a curse. Intrepid, my mother now telephoned Sarah, who at seventy-eight was single-handedly caring for her mother, Abuelita, 102. She was old now, Sarah. Perhaps there was a chink in the armor. She struck up a long conversation and secretly tape recorded it, mining a few nuggets of information. A story about the train to San Juan from Mayaguez that took them to the steamship Borinquen, and Sarah's great joy that day. Her terror when Leonor came back to New York for her daughter.

She wrote to her biological father, Felipe.

In his responding letter, he called Leonor a terrible mother who practiced *brujería*, left her children in hammocks, and ran around making merry. He said to never speak of this to anyone, and he underlined it twice. This made her want to print the letter in the *New York Times*.

I've seen pictures of the barrio in Mayaguez in the 1930s, of the tin roof house my Abuelita lived in before coming to America. It is dirt poor. The idea of Leonor running around in high heels and dancing for drinks is suspect.

No. The truth is, Felipe left for New York and married someone else. He promised to send for Leonor, and he never did. Then he gave his baby daughter to his sister Sarah and called it good. If it hadn't worked out, the women would have made it work out. It's a matriarchal culture among the Boricua. Men run off with other women to San Juan or Havana or Miami or New York. They run off to war, or to find work, or to the other end of the island. They don't bring wives or babies with them necessarily. They pick and choose. And sometimes, of course quite often, there is no choice. Poverty decides.

When Boricuas wish to keep a secret, they keep it. My mother has told me everything that she remembers. But Felipe took most of it to the grave. We do know Leonor died just before Felipe, was presumably waiting for him at Heaven's gate with their son. A little pissed, I imagine. Wearing a red dress, her black hair braided with seashells. Her baby not dead of starvation but fat and hale, on a silver throne.

I have the dog tag of Ferdinand Nunez, the good man who adopted my mother. A decorated soldier, he returned with medals to their apartment at 1568 Second Avenue in New York and died there when my mother was sixteen. The thin oblong of brass engraved with his name and address feels like a tiny safety shield on a silver chain around my neck.

Why did Leonor give her up? No one knows. She gave her up, and somehow my mother thrived without bitterness. Fifteen dollars was exchanged. Later my mother remarked, in her characteristic way of making something hard into something amusing, that even Judas Iscariot had gotten thirty pieces of silver. This was Bunny's alchemy. She made the tragic small, something she could step over like a stone.

Family lore has nineteen-year-old Leonor running to the train from Mayaguez at the last minute and handing over the baby before it pulled away. Because she knew her daughter would have a better life in New York. Because she loved another man. Because Felipe said he would send for her later. Because she needed those fifteen dollars. All things can be true. Great things can be terrible. Bad news can be good.

Born in 1917 in Lajas, Leonor is the biological grandmother I've never met. There is only her signature on my mother's birth certificate. One photograph on Ancestry.com, not validated but believed to be true. Large eyes, broad cheekbones, a wide nose. I see my mother and myself and my son Pablo. She swells. She winks.

Leonor visited Bunny just once in New York, and then she left, having failed in her mission to take her daughter back.

"She looked just like me," my mother said. "She wore a black dress and a cross necklace. She cried. I felt sorry for her."

"Everyone wanted me," she said. Flipping the narrative.

There is a hole in me, an unknown, and its name is Leonor. This hole is passed to my son and to his children and grandchildren. Yet when in crisis, I rely on Leonor for stealth and courage, something I feel she trafficked in all her life. I see her as a guardian of the underworld now, a figure made entirely of mystery and shadow, scorned and immensely powerful in her rage. She is not just the hole; she is the light inside me that no one sees.

When my mother's health began to decline in 2013, Tom and I flew west and took her and Ron to their favorite restaurant, Sizzler. Top sirloin, lime Jell-O. I asked her about Sarah and Felipe and Leonor, before she forgot all that she knew. I took her memories on my back, and I started walking toward this moment.

City of Angels

They moved to Los Angeles in the forties, my great grandmother Abuelita and her five surviving children and their children. My mother went to Van Nuys High School, home of the movie stars she would love all her life. Natalie Wood graduated just behind her, a woman who played a Puerto Rican on the big screen in *West Side Story*. My mother played one in real life.

One day Ferdinand's car broke down on the highway. A driver stopped, and they rushed forward gratefully in the summer heat. He waited until they were close then spat in their faces, calling them "dirty spics" as he sped away.

In Spanish there is a perfect expression, "Ni de aquí, ni de allá." *Not from here, not from there.* It's the national motto of Dementia.

Often now, my mother completely loses touch. *Ni de aquí, ni de allá.*
She always shifts back, and I am always deeply relieved. As though this is happening to me. As though I am not separate, was never born, and therefore need her here always. My host. Still, she travels, an invisible suitcase always at her side. A citizen of the wind.

Abuelita

Born in 1888, my great-grandmother Abuelita's two-room shack in Mayaguez housed her and her husband Sixto and eight children, including twins who died of malnutrition in infancy, Daniel and John. They all slept on the floor.

She worked nights, ironing men's shirts for a few pennies. In the yard behind the house, she planted vegetables and peanuts, which she'd roast and trade for food in the small market. Her daughter Sarah and her son Felipe would go to the beach and gather sand crabs, which Abuelita made into soup. In 1937, she brought her children and granddaughter to New York, saving their lives. She was deeply revered and cared for at home by Sarah until the day she died at 105. Sarah would stand in front of her mother's chair and draw her to her feet, then turn around. Abuelita would hang on, spooning her body from behind. Slowly, they would cross to the kitchen to eat *sopa de pollo* and play cards. To the bathroom. To the bedroom. A human walker. A Pushmepullyou going in the same direction.

My people don't crack under pressure. They grow a thicker skin, like dragons. The better to fly.

I last saw Abuelita at Sarah's house in Arleta when she was 100. When I looked into her eyes, it was all there.

This is who I come from. This is who I am.

Ponce de Leon the Butcher

Most Americans don't realize Puerto Rico is a colonial territory, nor did they ever. Even fewer know that Columbus "discovered" Puerto Rico during his second voyage. Puerto Ricans are direct descendants of the people Columbus brutalized. Ponce de Leon was in one of Columbus's exploration parties. Now, *he* was a butcher. Ponce de Leon made Columbus look like Gandhi.

Ponce de Leon didn't discover, as we learned in elementary school, the fountain of youth. He discovered a fountain of fresh Taino slaves. Which was good, he felt, because Spain was running out. The new slaves laid blue cobblestones throughout the streets of San Juan, or else they were slain with machetes.

Things went from bad to worse as Puerto Rico fell into the clutches of the United States the year my Abuelita was born in 1898. As the years went by, much of the real tradition and history was swept neatly under the rug of U.S. Sugar, the bubbling colonialist one-pot meal that Truman made of the island.

Later there was a Puerto Rican Nationalist attack on the White House, led by a woman named Lolita LeBrón. *Bruja*, no doubt.

This partially explains why many Boricuas never go back to the island. There is a thin film of genocide there. *Let's go back to the butcher* is not a refrain one often hears in the streets of New York or Los Angeles, then or now.

But when the five PR Nationalists were let out of jail after twenty-six years, they went to Casa Adela on the lower east side of Manhattan. They had some authentic Caribe food. Then they returned home.

But they had to go back. The rest do not.

Not one of my family has.

License

Today, I find my mother's driver's licenses in a little pile in her office drawer. I pocket them. Height 5'2". Weight 140. Hair Blk. Eyes Brn. Such small details; such common attributes. Why do I weep? It's the leopard print coat I see her wearing. It's the white headband, so plain and innocent, like a girl's. It's the different address on each driver's license because money was tight, and we had to move a lot, though she made it seem right, always a step up. These are appreciative tears. Water of love.

She learned to drive after my father left so that she didn't have to ride the bus to work, transferring at Fruitvale. She was afraid; she was thirty-five, but she learned. Ron bought her an ancient Ford with extensive rust damage. We called it The Green Bomb and put large daisy stickers on it. It was the seventies. Were we hippies? We were. Look at her black eyeliner with a wing on each eye. Look at the defiant expression as she smiles for the DMV, her hair curled tight in a natural. Note the additional addresses on the back of each driver's license, as she wound her way through Oakland neighborhoods, a swag lamp in each apartment, taking her two children and her second, younger husband along.

My grandmother Sarah drove until she was forced to stop at ninety. She had shrunk to 4'10" and needed a pillow on the car seat as she tooled through the streets of Arleta,

California, an upbeat multilingual woman with a vanity plate that said RUFINA, Abuelita's name. She was too short and too old to drive, but she placed a bolster on the car seat and rode on. She came from Depression dirt floors and needed to stay mobile. Something might come again that would need driving away from.

I have Sarah's last driver license as well. It's right here.

Now I am the only driver, the last driver. Born in 1935, my mother is the last Boricua.

I put the driver's licenses away. In my hands, the slim plastic cards feel powerful. A license to something more.

Cleaning the living room, I discover my mother's purse, tucked behind the piano bench of the dusty baby grand she doesn't play anymore, which sits like a bad tooth in the corner, collecting detritus.

"Is there anything in it?" Ron says.

A keychain from Disneyland: I LOVE GRANDMA. A monogrammed triple lipstick case I gave her, red leather. **BOM** Bunny Olga Mathews. Her fourth name. Her fourth life.

Some tissues. A small black velvet case with miniature tarot cards inside for emergency on-the-go divination. I pocket this. I will draw one card every time I am sad and divine the solution. Reason has no quarter here.

One tattered fabric wallet, with appointment cards from Kaiser and AARP. Some blank checks. A comb. Herbal cough drops, loose.

I hand Ron back the purse, cloth with a Navajo pattern. I hand it back, thinking that to discard it in front of him would overstep.

I don't keep everything I want to keep; I don't live in the Taj Mahal. But this is hard. This is her purse. I take it home.

The Rescue

The millennium had just arrived. My son was born. My husband left. Another woman.

And here comes Bunny, a warrior in polyester pants and oval sunglasses. On a wave of love she comes, on a speeding fire engine with lights ablaze, on a winged chariot from Hayward she comes, bearing urns of light.

My mother sits on the brown chair opposite me, creating a zone. An island of healing and consideration, outside of time.

I am on the couch, flying apart.

She watches me smoke. Cracks open a paperback, carefully places the elaborate bookmark aside. Says wise things. Laughs at my prophecies of doom. How I will never love again. How my baby son will wither in his soul.

"I want to die," I say. "I want him to die."

They are the same thing, to me.

"Los hombres nunca mueren cuando tú quieres," she says.

Men never die when you want them to.

Destiny

My mother believed deeply in fate and visualization and all forms of magic, telling me that someday I would be published, despite decades of rejections and passes.

"It's your destiny," she would say.

When my novel sold for publication, she was not surprised, but instead asked me what was next. A story of our family?

Later, I said. *We'll write it together.*

In 2000, she predicted I would have three children. When I pointed out that I was forty-one and divorced, she said, *I have seen it.*

In 2010, I married Tom. He had two young children. Now we were five. I was living in North Carolina and in the thick of it again. I didn't notice as her mind slid sideways, and she stopped emailing me or engaging in complex conversations. Her personality stayed the same. She was always cheerful and upbeat, born to land on her feet and heal what she could—until she turned eighty, and the earth shifted, and one day, without preamble, she landed in a wholly different country.

Cinderella Trail

I am walking on the Cinderella Trail in the Oakland Hills. The beauty slaps me in the face.

I think about how you never see an oak wishing it were a sequoia or an old tree wishing it were young again. It revels and grows even as it twists, always toward the sky. Sometimes they may grow perpendicular to the ground, but not for long— they rise up. They let go of things when it's time and have faith in the regeneration of seasons. You never see a tree wishing it were somewhere else. It just doesn't happen.

Some dogs pass with their owners. One is very old with a white muzzle. My dog Colette cowers. She fears everything unless she is behind our locked door, and then she raises Hell.

More and more I see it may be necessary to have some legitimate faith, not just California mumbo jumbo, such as "Stay safe...I have a pink bubble around your truck, enjoy the wine country!" and "That butterfly was a sign from Grama."

I resolve to go back to Saint Andrew in Marin City, the wonderfully diverse church I attended during my divorce years, having learned about it from Anne Lamott's books.

To sustain myself as I follow Bunny into Dementia, I have needed a great many books, spoken aloud for ease of digestion. But mostly, I require a pit crew, a consortium, a tiny circus of people to hold me down and speak bald truth and scathing irreverence. Without them, I would be doomed to wander the swamps of self-pity and resentment and reside in a deep depression in the earth. Landscapes such as this make up the lion's share of Dementia. Here I advise fellow travelers: gather your Greek chorus. Keep them close.

Best Friend

Her name is Dee. Our connection intensifies each day we live. Her mind melded with mine, by osmosis, during homeroom of seventh grade, which is where we met. She was with me in the A–F section of the alphabet, in that quadrant of the Oakland public school universe. I lean on her.

Looking into her face is like looking into a clear sky. I breathe better, know I am known. It's what I imagine a blood sister would feel like.

What else is she? The receptacle for my memories. The touchstone I touch to know where I am. The filter I run my life through for texture analysis. She is the Obi-Wan Kenobi figure in the corner with a hoodie and a dark look. She is also the ebullient court jester with the colorful tights who can leap through the air and make me laugh in the midst of anything, anywhere.

We speak in half sentences. Just before she says something, I get a mental flash of what she is about to say, what topic we have now switched to. We switch topics swiftly, creating a kinetic blur. We talk over one another and still hear every word. We have an entire secret language, consisting of phrases, acronyms, and facial expressions, able to convey a whole complete narrative in a trice. We are like primates signing to one another while the world looks on and wonders what exactly we are doing.

I have a video of the day we graduated from middle school. I am wearing a long, diaphanous white halter dress with deep red roses and forest green leaves. There is a little matching jacket to the dress, which falls to the ground and has ruffles along the bottom hem and at the hem of the jacket. Her tall and stately older sister Danielle loaned me that dress. The video is a time tunnel and a magic carpet to the past.

Now in her sixties, she is wise but still cares about all the petty things, and for that, I admire her. When I saw her last Christmas, she made crêpes from Serbia, *palacinke*, stuffed with dark chocolate, raspberries, and cinnamon sugar. Now whenever I picture her dancing in my kitchen and waving her magic rusty crêpe pan, I exhale. Come back to center.

Child Review

"Do you think you and Tom will have children?" my mother asks confidingly.

"I'm sixty-two, Mom," I say.

"What? That's terrible."

"Oh, I know."

I explain that between us, we have three children, ages thirteen, nineteen, and twenty-three. I go through them one by one. I do a Child Review.

"So, we already have enough," I say in summation.

Her eyes cloud. The window shuts.

My mother won't willingly let anyone touch her or care for her except myself and Ron. She was sexually abused by her uncle when she was seven. She's never had a massage, has never worn a bathing suit or learned to swim. She grew big after menopause and settled into a life without the attention of men. Now she is small, a size that would have been appealing and therefore dangerous. But she is safe now. No pedophiles visit Dementia.

Causes

What caused this? Your once-fine brain, poured onto the floor. Was it blood pressure? Weight? Diet Coke? Was it the Prozac you needed after your hysterectomy? Twenty years, you were on it. A mistake, they know now.

Was it hair dye? Was it some box you opened, or didn't open?

Not a disease, but a gang of symptoms. Slippery. Manifold. *Mixed Dementia*, the doctors think. Not Alzheimer's. An autopsy would tell us, but no.

There was a box, and somehow it was opened, and this spilled out, staining all the world. You didn't know. Pandora was only curious. Created by the gods, like you. The first woman, as you were to me. Beautiful, deceitful, stubborn, cunning— yet pure. Not to be blamed for what has happened. Tricked by the gods.

If told never to open a box, you must.

Church

Before the 1960s spirited my father away with counterculture wings, Richard was a Baptist minister in San Francisco. He wore a dark suit and was cleanshaven then: no beard, no hair curling

25

down and touching his collar, no smell of whiskey. I remember getting dressed for church with white patent leather shoes. When I was three, he baptized me. I remember that as well. Being dipped in a little white ceramic tub, just my face being splashed with water. His face above mine. Feeling safe. This was how it was done, I assumed. Everyone did this.

Today I am at Saint Andrew Presbyterian Church in Marin City. Reverend Floyd Thompkins is a big Black man with a dashiki and a preacher's voice. When he sees me walk in, he opens his arms. I walk into them. Another father, younger than me this time. I am held in fragrant grace, just the scent of soap and skin.

This Sunday's Invocation is, *let our worship increase our faith expand our vision and soothe our souls. Surrounded by darkness, we come to bask in the light and the love of God.*

The Passing of the Peace comes first. I hug everyone. The indiscriminate nature of the affection is bracing. Nothing is weighed out or meted.

May the peace of the Lord be with you. And also with you.

During the service, he flails his arms and advises us to love our neighbor as ourselves. We laugh with him. We sing. A line of sweat trickles down his face and he cries out.

God, he says, *makes a way of no way.*

In my experience, He does, but it is never the way we envisioned. He is a tricky bastard.

COVID-19 means a lot of people on a Zoom monitor and a dozen or so in the folding chairs. When the beautiful soulful woman plays the piano on Zoom, we sing with her. There is a technical glitch, and her audio is silenced. We continue to sing. The words to the hymns are right there on the screen. *Steal*

Away. I Surrender All. Fix Me, Jesus. I clap and croon, my voice in several wrong keys.

During Silent Confession, I confess. Where I have envied. Where I have lacked faith. As always, I run out of time to get to half of it.

Pastor Floyd leads the Call to Prayer.

> *Come Holy Spirit and invade our thoughts and emotions with the passion of optimism, inexhaustible joy, and inexplicable assurance that everything will be all right.*
>
> *Despite discouragement, give us undeniable optimism that God is still at work.*

During the prayer offering I go to the microphone and ask for prayers for Bunny. I try not to cry, but I do. As I walk back to my seat, two people touch my arm. I feel the Holy Spirit, a zing of love passing from them to me, a kind of electricity. A protective shield, light as breath.

Brothers

My brother hasn't seen or spoken to our mother since 2016.

There's a wall I run up against when I try to write about my brother. A layer of skin I must cut through, even estranged. We were close as children, just three years apart, but not since. There are no others, save the brothers I fashioned out of friends: my writer friend, Augusten; my childhood friend, Rob; my creative partner, Ken.

After my divorce, my brother took time out of his day to compose a letter, a diatribe. He was on the side of my ex-husband, even though they too never spoke.

I blocked him with a kind of happiness. I created a bubble around him and stored him away with childhood. I kissed him tenderly and placed him on a rocket to the sun.

In my mother's house, there are pictures of him, of us, in frames. Weekly, I visit the museum of the dead past.

When his face appears on the Parade of Faces, his elegant hand holding a wine glass, my mother says nothing, and I say nothing. I am hoping she has forgotten him, and so has forgotten his abandonment. All hail Dementia.

I've saved his Baby Book and his report cards. The first Christmas ornament he made out of a cardboard toilet paper roll, painted green and doused in glitter. When I come across other little inconsequential things that I suspect he would want, I hesitate and then throw them away. There are bridges you never cross twice.

Pool of Truth

I met Augusten by email in 1990, when he left his job as a copywriter in San Francisco, and his boss hired me. She said, *You two should know each other*, and gave him my email. We shared everything from that day on; no matter what, we said it. We called it the Pool of Truth. We made that for one another. A sanctuary. He became my jackpot brother, the steady one I never had.

I talk to him today and say it has been heartbreaking to watch Bunny decline, but so be it. There is no avoidance.

"Yes," he says. "You are supposed to drive straight through the center of it all."

"Exactly," I say. "And well-meaning people keep trying to make it into a happy story or a homily. The word *closure* and other yellow ribbon fallacies are being rained upon me, which is maddening."

"Yes, there will be no closure," Augusten says. "You are being spared not being there and imagining. You get to take inventory of all you are losing."

"I would have been much better off with a Rican mother," he goes on to say. "Mine was so totally useless. She gave me away to an insane man who read turds as a fortune-telling device and then abused me."

I tell him that a Rican mother would have driven to that house and beaten that man to death using her *caldero* rice pot... which is aluminum so that it seeps into the brain bit by bit and makes us even crazier than we were originally.

"I worry about aluminum..." Then he pivots. "I love that she died without getting any of me. I published *Running with Scissors* and never saw or spoke to her again."

"I love the aluminum," I say. "I also love the uranium-red Fiestaware. The more it damages me? The better I float."

"You have to use all this," he says.

Two years ago, Augusten announced that I must write about losing my mother while she's still here. I confessed I was in despair.

"I dream of her," I told him. "I see her gliding around like a ghost. But she's still alive."

"In a horrible way, it will be a relief," he told me. "It was better after my grandmother was dead than when she was alive but mostly dead."

"Begin. Slap it together however," he said. "Let randomness enter, Bwaby."

"I am so worn out and old," I said.

"Why are you taking a self-pity bath when you have a book to write?"

The Seven Stages

In Dementia, the land is divided not into states, but stages.

Stage 1: No significant problems with memory. No cognitive impairment.

Stage 2: Occasional lapses of memory. Forgetting where one has placed an object. Forgetting names that were once very familiar. At this stage, signs are still virtually undetectable through clinical testing.

Stage 3: Clear cognitive problems begin to manifest. Getting lost easily. Noticeably poor performance at work. Forgetting the names of family members and close friends. Difficulty retaining information read in a book or passage. Losing or misplacing important objects.

Stage 4: Decreased knowledge of current and/or recent events. Difficulty remembering things about one's personal history. Decreased ability to handle finances or arrange travel plans.

Stage 5: Inability to remember major details such as the name of a close family member. Disorientation about the time and place. Forgets basic information about themselves, such as a telephone number or address. Patients need assistance with basic functions such as using the bathroom or eating. Patients still have the ability to remember their own names and generally the names of spouses and children.

Stage 6: When the patient begins to forget the names of their children, spouse, or primary caregivers, they are most

likely entering Stage 6 of dementia and will need full-time care. Caregivers and loved ones should watch for delusional behavior, obsessive behavior, and symptoms of anxiety, aggression, agitation, wandering, difficulty sleeping, and hallucinations.
Stage 7: In the final stage, the brain seems to lose its connection with the body. Loss of all motor skills and verbal abilities.

By identifying the earliest stages of dementia in the patient as they occur, you may be able to seek medical treatment quickly and delay the onset of later stages.
Dementia is irreversible and incurable.

My mother is Stage Seven. She is not a patient; she is a woman in a foreign land.
Also? They buried the lede.

A Nimbus of Blurred Space

On her birthday, I sense my grandma, Sarah, in the house. The air around the bed is different; it thickens. And I feel something, a very specific presence. The scent of cotton twice ironed.

It's tempting to think I imagine the whole thing, but Bunny would see it differently. She would say, *Yes, I just felt her this morning, in the kitchen. Near the stove.*

My mother would supply for me the exact, specific area where the nimbus of blurred space appeared.

This sort of thing has been happening to our people for centuries. The veil between the worlds is like cheesecloth with Boricua. There may as well be no veil at all.

My Mother's Abortion

It was 1966. Bunny was separated from my father, and he didn't want it. There was no money.

She had to prove she was mentally unfit to have a baby in order to have an abortion. She answered a series of questions, telling the truth and telling lies.

Ron was already in my mother's life, and so she asked him to drive her to the hospital. She didn't tell him why.

I remember the robe she was wearing when my dad brought her home from the hospital. It was turquoise blue and red, quilted, floor length. It was new, which made it conspicuous. A gift. Then he left for his apartment in the tenderloin district of San Francisco.

They told her it was a boy. She never got over it. She had her tubes tied at thirty-one—to close the portal.

But now she has forgotten it. Now she is wiped clean. Shriven.

There is a powerful, indiscriminate wind that blows through Dementia, sweeping away the painful past but also whisking away the last few minutes, leaving a tabula rasa. There is vast destruction but also mercy. Choose where to look. Pace yourself; the way is long.

Key Facts

The World Health Organization, September 2021

> *Dementia is a syndrome—usually of a chronic or progressive, nature—that leads to deterioration in cognitive function.*
>
> *Consciousness is not affected.*

Worldwide, around 55 million people have dementia, with over 60% living in low- and middle-income countries. As the proportion of older people in the population is increasing in nearly every country, this number is expected to rise to 78 million in 2030 and 139 million in 2050.

Dementia is currently the seventh leading cause of death among all diseases and one of the major causes of disability and dependency among older people worldwide.

There is currently no treatment available to cure dementia, though numerous new treatments are being investigated in various stages of clinical trials.

Globally, dementia has a disproportionate impact on women. Additionally, women provide the majority of informal care for people living with dementia, accounting for 70% of career hours.

Unfortunately, people with dementia are frequently denied the basic rights and freedoms available to others. In many countries, physical and chemical restraints are used extensively.

Studies show that people can reduce their risk of cognitive decline and dementia by being physically active, not smoking, avoiding harmful use of alcohol, controlling their weight, eating a healthy diet, and maintaining healthy blood pressure, cholesterol and blood sugar levels. Additional risk factors include depression, social isolation, low educational attainment, cognitive inactivity and air pollution.[1]

---

[1] "Dementia," World Health Organization, March 15, 2023, https://www.who.int/news-room/fact-sheets/detail/dementia.

Takeaways From the Key Facts

Don't get old. Don't get depressed. Don't drink. Don't smoke. Don't take drugs. Don't be sedentary. Don't be poor. Don't be less than brilliant. Don't forgo college. Don't be stressed. Don't have high blood pressure or cholesterol. Don't eat sugar, don't eat salt. Don't eat cookies, don't fry chicken. Don't be idle. Don't live alone. Don't contract HIV. Don't hit your head on anything. Don't be battered. Don't live in foreign countries, or else you'll be tortured. Don't live in this country. Don't be a woman. Don't breathe the air. Best wishes, and remember this: *You will be saved by family or not at all.*

A Great Day

It was an accident of the light that made it seem as though my father was standing just behind my left shoulder in the closet full-length mirror. I see now it was a plaid jacket hanging on a hook. I feel ready to see ghosts these days.

I look at myself in profile and think that my butt is creeping up my back. It is literally sneaking up on me. Or it may be my back fat is settling down into my rear. I step forward and look at my face without giving myself the raised eyebrow Botox expression of surprise and allure. I just let my features sag all the way in. I instantly become my mother.

And why not? She and I are in this together, marching to the beat of time. Parallel souls on a parallel journey, working to surrender to the One.

I don't believe the dead actually come back, but that doesn't stop them from laying a finger on a shoulder, a waviness in the air, a shimmering, a thickening. A quickening. Something recreating itself, but only partially, just enough to see without losing your mind. A reflection in the toaster, a shape like him but unlike him.

When a loved one dies, they linger. We hear them smoking, laughing, agreeing, or disagreeing, making irreverent remarks, quipping in our mind. In some ways, they're more real to us than the living.

I didn't really believe my father could die. It was a physical affront that hid something much worse behind its back, and that is grief.

Grief. A shape shifter, an instigator, a raving toddler, a magi, a vehicle to reach the other side. There is no love without this.

Bunny used to say that we don't die inadvertently. We plan it. It's the flourish on our signature.

My father chose a dramatic death with his third wife, who I adored, whose chocolate Mayan eyes were a beautiful window to her gritty, immaculate soul, a woman who cooked like the wind. He is here in spirit forever, but what good is that? Can he help with my mother? Can he calm my fears? No, he cannot now nor did he ever, once he disappeared into the bottle. For that matter, what exactly did he do in life? He preached. He drank. He had three wives. He died on a highway when I was a teenager. And ever since, I have been searching for some important coda, some grand sweeping thing he did to emerge, some valiant, secret deed that will erase all else.

It's a great day when you stop waiting for the thing that is never going to happen.

But these details are just his rap sheet. There is more. He gave my mother two children to love. He gave us his sense of humor. He once marched with Dr. Martin Luther King Jr., representing his church in Selma. He showed us what caring deeply and what not caring looked like, and what its cost might be. And he gave me life. If that was the only thing he did, I can honor him. I can start right now. I can lay down my dead father. I can stop keeping score.

I never see my father Richard or my stepmother Gayle, of course, not even in dreams. I feel, however, that they are out there, like telephone poles, stray dogs, just out there. They fly beyond my visage. Yet I am not above seeing things. Right now, I think a small pile of clothes on a chair to my right is a dog, but it's not. I think the bar of light under the door is illumined dread, seeping into my room. I think my face in the mirror has a second and third face, the face of a child and a crone.

Many times, after my father left home and drank his way to oblivion, I wished him gone. And that seemed sad but real and necessary. But now that he's dead, he's finally here again. His essence pours through the windows like sunshine.

The Bullshit Window

My ex-husband and I are texting today.

When he left me, his mistress was many years younger than I was. This was like a physical blow. When I told my mother her age, she was in her kitchen slicing apples for a cake.

"Anyone can be young. It's not an achievement in and of itself," Bunny said.

"But not anyone," she said, sliding the apples off her knife, "can be old."

Was she planning on putting a small curse on the woman? I waited eagerly.

"One good thing?" I told her. "When your divorce is final, and you live two thousand miles apart? The bullshit window is closed."

"No, it's not," Bunny says, folding vanilla into the bowl of apples.

"What?"

"It's not." She cuts some butter into the flour. "The relationship goes on."

"You're always there with the Good News, aren't you, Mom?"

She was right, of course.

I used to hang on to my anger with Mark, but it was like walking around with a paper bag on my head for a decade. So, I took it off.

Now my ex and I are texting about onions. He used to microwave them, grill them with chunky kosher salt on top, then splash with balsamic vinegar. I need to know, white onions or yellow? Would red onions work? He says they would.

After Mark left, and he came to see Pablo every Saturday morning, he would drink coffee with cream and raw sugar at the kitchen table. I would also drink coffee. It became something we would do together instead of being married.

And he did come to see Pablo, often. Mark had left me, not Pablo, a fact he felt compelled to point out when I suggested early on that he and his girlfriend move to Zambia. But he couldn't and wouldn't be far from his son. So, we went from a family of three people who could go anywhere to four people bound to one place, but never the same place at the same time. It was a game of psychic Twister.

Then his girlfriend turned up pregnant. I rolled with that little shiv to the ribs too.

It put paid to all thought of reconciliation.

In fact, in the moment he told me about the baby, I felt a pain in the center of my chest like a battering ram. Then I stopped. I thought about it. I tamped my broken heart down, and I switched into a lower gear. I chuckled long and low, right in his face. He was going to be one of those dads with white hair and a little limp.

Then I got very brisk and very busy taking everything I had previous felt unentitled to…little things of his. You impregnate a younger woman? I take your grandfather's pocket watch. You want to borrow Pablo's old crib? I resist the temptation to leave a voodoo doll under the layette, but I do sequester your favorite Bowie knife in a secret place you will never find.

The new normal crept in like the dog that it was.

If it had been up to me? Ten minutes after he told me she was pregnant, I would have finalized the divorce. The baby made that easy. The perfect coda.

It is very hard to keep loving someone who loves someone else. It made me feel greasy.

But on those Saturdays when Mark came to visit Pablo, I would let him in, and we always had coffee. In fact, I made the coffee, pushing the button on the machine the moment I heard his car in the driveway, a familiar sound. A sound like a kind of sonar to my insides. Still.

I will tell you another still. I still liked watching his face while he drank the coffee. I liked the way it settled into itself.

I wonder if the girlfriend knew about the coffee. I wonder if I made the coffee to spite her. Later, I stopped making coffee just for him. But then, he had stopped loving me. I wonder if everything comes out even. I would settle for even.

Favorite Curse

In the before time, Bunny's favorite curse was *Se cosecha lo que se siembra.* As you sow so shall you reap. You go out as you come in. You will die as you have lived. She watched Telenovela shows that constantly proved her point. She would be entranced by a rerun of *Dos Mujeres, Un Camino* (*Two Women, One Path*) with Eric Estrada starring as big rig truck driver Johnny Villegas, perpetually torn between two women. She loved Johnny Villegas, despite his predictably fiendish ways with women.

"It's not just the Latinos…" Bunny said, "…but the Latinos are the worst. Antonio Banderas had a beautiful Spanish wife. He meets Melanie Griffith, who decides he's hers now. Antonio leaves the wife. Then he does Melanie the same. Now she's ruined her face."

Se cosecha lo que se siembra. It's not even a curse, really. It's pointing out the efficacy of the curse that already exists out there in the psychic troposphere, where good and bad weather occurs, where an account is taken of all that is said and done.

She said that even just idly saying "Se cosecha lo que se siembra" is in and of itself a light, almost invisible spell.

Use wisely, said she.

I speak almost no Spanish. Knowing some words and phrases is not the same.

My father did not ban Spanish, but he did not encourage it or learn it himself. By the time he died, I was past the osmosis stage of language absorption. I was well into the intellectually lazy self I perfected just one day after college graduation.

Not only did my father begrudge me the beauty of that language, but he also made it seem like a second-class language. So even though I wanted to learn Spanish so I could understand my relatives, English always seemed more important, the one to master. I won spelling bees. I memorized grammar doctrines. I scored high on written/verbal SATs.

I see now I was wrong. About not just this, but many things that matter. Otherwise, I would not be ignorant and unable to say the Spanish word for *onion*.

Cebolla, Google Translator says.

In a perfect world, my father would have embraced his wife's language. But he didn't, nor did many other husbands of other Ricans. As for my mother's family, they were linguists. They had to learn English and learn it well to function, and they knew some other Spanish dialects as well. As soon as my father walked into the room, they all easily switched to English.

My parents were happily married. I can remember that. My father was a good father before he left; I remember that. He carried me on his shoulders, he taught me to swim and ride a bike, and then he died. I felt safe beside him right up until the time he left us. But we were not close.

He never learned a word of Spanish, and he did not want Bunny to speak Spanish in front of him, as though it was a crude act. He felt it was rude for the family as well, so they spoke English.

I don't know what to add to this except to say that I think he felt outnumbered, and in truth, he was. Yet, I regret I didn't absorb the language growing up; I could have simply breathed it in, like deep rich oxygen.

In a perfect world, I would speak fluent Spanish and, more importantly, understand the most beautiful language in the world. It's not a perfect world, and I don't. And the sum effect of not speaking Spanish is feeling like I am not really Puerto Rican, and I am not white either: *Ni de aqui, ni de alla.*

"Well, you can speak anything once you die and move on," Dee says. "I wouldn't worry about it if I were you."

Acronyms R Us

Dee and I speak in acronyms. It started with us making an acronym out of a little thing we would do with our faces when we were especially pleased or needed to emphasize a statement. We would move our jaw sideways and raise our eyebrows. We named it Jaw Movement, then shortened it to JM and included it in writing notes to each other in school, and it went from there. We frequent all the usual ones (BRB, TY, TTYS, TTYL, FOMO) but have added some others.

OOB. Out of body.

OFB. Open for business.

FAFFing. Fucking Around Forever, the act of.

TYSK is the one we use most, used while texting random facts, apropos of nothing: *Thought You Should Know.* As in, *Mangos are ten for $10 at Lucky's. TYSK. Pablo is dating a girl named Neptune. TYSK. My eyebrows are going in two separate directions, now. TYSK.*

IBY. I Blame You. Ever so handy in almost every confession.

POTP. Part of the Problem.

POTP can be used ubiquitously. I use it often. I slide it in under my breath, passive aggressively. As always, the harder I look at my problems, the more I see that I am POTP.

ELD. *Every little detail.* Example: *Call me and give me ELD on the _____. Can't wait for ELD. I'll ELD you later.*

ILYAEAY. *I love you and everything about you.*

OTT. *Over the top.*

RSC. *Radical self-care.*

IRL. *In Real Life.* As in, *You have to meet him IRL, not just on Bumble.*

Today, Dee and I are FAFFING and listening to *Practicing the Power of Now* by Eckhart Tolle (ET). He doesn't talk from a script; he just babbles. Every so often, he rings a Tibetan singing bowl.

"If you delve into the past, it will become a bottomless pit. There's always more," he says.

"Like potato chips…" Dee says sagely.

ET has much to say about time and what to do with it. I listen carefully.

"When you catch yourself slipping into waiting, snap out of it. Come into the present moment. If you are present, there's never any need to wait for anything. Just be and enjoy being. But beware, the false unhappy self, based on mind identification lives on time. It knows that the present moment is its own death and so feels very threatened by it. It will try to keep you trapped in time."

TFUSBOMI is my new favorite thing. *The False Unhappy Self Based on Mind Identification.*

"It's not the easiest acronym to remember," Dee says. "TFUS is nice, though. The False Unhappy Self. BOMI is also good. Based on Mind Identification. Maybe they work separately."

"TFUSBOMI. It really trips off the tongue…" I say, undeterred. "TEEE FUSS BO MEEEE."

A longer acronym can be like a full sentence, I explain to her. It is complete in and of itself.

"Well. I love TFUS," she affirms. "And FUS is like fuss, so. *The End.*"

Dee and I say *The End* at the end of any declarative thought.

BlacKkKlansman *deserved the Oscar, and* Green Book *was shit.* The End.

No matter how slimming it is, we're too old to wear all black now. We need something lightly colored near our faces. The End.

Al Pacino needs to cut his hair. The End.

Sourdough toast is a complete meal. The End

When we were nineteen, we went to a psychic fair in Berkeley. There were healing booths, card reading booths, and so much more. You could get your chakras cleansed for only five dollars.

Our tarot card reader's name was Mala Kabala. She wore thick eyeliner and was, in all respects, a caricature of a false prophet. The dyed hair, the cheap bangles. The flamboyant personality coupled with hoop earrings and a long flowing skirt. All of it.

She told me I would have three children. For decades, I thought, *Well, she got that wrong. What a farce.*

Eastman Street

Last night, I dreamt I went to Eastman Street, where our family lived in the 1960s. The low cyclone metal fence around the house stood still, its rusted gate latched and padlocked. I heard dogs barking, but no dog could harm me, a dreamer. The loquat trees bore no fruit. The blackberry brambles had triumphed in the end, strangling them at the base. It seemed to me that my parent's marriage lay in the ruined yard.

I knew that I dreamed. I walked the perimeters, noting the changes. The apple and pear trees in the backyard had been cut down in favor of a small rental unit. No more homemade applesauce with chunks of pear.

I will not tell Bunny this dream. Best to not bring the past springing back to life any more than it already is.

"Think of time as a continuum," Augusten says. "I beg of you."

I'm not sure what he means. I look up the word.

Continuum

1. A continuous sequence in which adjacent elements are not perceptibly different from each other, although the extremes are quite distinct.
2. Mathematics: The set of real numbers.

Who Do You Belong To?

"Who do you belong to?" Bunny asks me today. Truculent.

"You, Mommy. I belong to you." I say.

She turns away.

I am cleaning the living room, where she and Ron have twin adjustable beds they rarely leave, like the grandparents in *Willy Wonka & the Chocolate Factory*.

A few minutes go by.

"Do you want us to drive you home?" my mother asks.

The bum's rush. Ron and I laugh. Humor is our primary defense.

"No, seriously," she says, and then turns on Ron, who is on the loveseat crammed in the corner.

"Why are you sitting over there?" she demands.

"There's nowhere else to sit," he says.

"There are plenty of places to sit…" my mother says, gesturing grandly around the tiny room.

Who do I belong to now?

Imposter

But you don't understand, I want to say. *My mother is a dynamo. My mother worked overtime and never let us know we were on the brink. My mother dressed up as a clown for Halloween, and she went all the way. She got the clown shoes, and she wore them. My mother came to me and my baby when my husband left, and she willed me back into existence. My mother could answer the phone and fix whatever was on the other side, using only her voice and sense of humor.*

You don't understand, I want to say. *This is an imposter.*

Is there a room in Dementia where they keep the real mothers and grandmothers? Will they reveal themselves if we decide we have had enough of these imposters? Because I can wait. I have all day.

Liz Taylor

I am of medium height, sturdy, my complexion dark and inconsistent. In summer, I appear coffee, and in winter, I am almost green. Twenty minutes in the sun, and I go eggplant. I never burn. Like all the women in my family, I am short waisted and will never run out of hair. None of our people do. I'm aging nominally well, like a cheese. On a good day, I get the same acclaim as cheese. But I will eventually become shrunken and compressed like Abuelita. I must face it because in my family,

45

there are examples of me all around, wizening. Growing smaller yet more powerful.

As a child, I inwardly apologized for my knees, which are of a darker color than the rest of me; there is a smudge of ash where my elbows point as well. I wanted the smooth pink knees of Vicki Whitman, the pearl knees of Penny Godwin. I wanted my arms and legs to be all one color, preferably a light creamy one. But sometime in the eighties, brown women came into fashion. Soon, white women were getting sprayed with dark color. I was pre-sprayed by Jesus.

Things work out sometimes. For a while.

You wouldn't call me pretty, and growing up, people made a point of telling me this, as though to warn me of something. I always looked different, my face too much bone and too round all at once. I got my period before everyone; I was ten. I grew faster than everyone, and then I stopped. In the end, it was more a stateliness that came through, and something I'd learned from my mother: a determination to be attractive. My mother decided to be the most beautiful woman in any room before she entered it. *And so I was*, she said. *You are what you project*, she said.

My mom loved Liz Taylor: she had black hair, she was low to the ground, and she buried a lot of men. Liz Taylor is an honorary Boricua. Decades ago, I called Liz Taylor "old," and Bunny gave me a filthy look.

Later, I saw Liz Taylor on *Entertainment Tonight*, and she said, "There's never a *time* to give up. You decide that. You make that happen."

I will try to listen to Bunny and Liz Taylor. They are the brave scouts who went ahead to forge a path for me.

Exit, January 1979

Today, I find a newspaper clipping in my mother's office.

Survivors Of Accident Killed While Viewing Wreckage

REDDING (AP) Three survivors who had just survived the rollover of their pickup truck were killed by a logging truck as they stood in the road, says the California Highway Patrol.

The report said that late Sunday on Highway 273 south of Redding, the south-bound pickup truck, whose headlights had gone out, swerved to avoid a van entering the highway.

The occupants of the pickup truck, unhurt, were surveying the wreckage when the logging truck came along, the CHP said.

The dead were identified as Ivan Brown, thirty-nine, of nearby Anderson, and Donald R. Finnamore, forty-three, and Gayle Finnamore, thirty-two, both of San Francisco.

The logging truck driver was identified as Murray Gene Grady, fifty-two, of Red Bluff, who suffered minor injuries. The CHP said the pickup driver was Joseph Valenzuela of Oakland. No citations were immediately issued.[2]

It was December 31. Twilight. The most dangerous time of day on the most dangerous day. A signature move, for my father.

It wasn't a pickup truck; it was a Jeep with room for five. Ivan and his wife Jane had just been married in his flat on Chestnut Street. This was their honeymoon.

When I went to collect his belongings, the decorations were still up.

CONGRATULATIONS. A paper heart banner across the kitchen.

---

[2] "Survivors Of Accident Killed While Viewing Wreckage," *The Sacramento Bee,* January 2, 1979.

The Jeep rolled. His best friend Joe ran up the road to signal cars out of the lane with a red bandana. Only Ivan turned to see the logging truck speeding toward them. He pushed his wife Jane out of the way, saving her life in the instant his ended. They were knocked thirty-five feet. Bowling pins.

In the police photographs, which I am instructed not to look at, I see my father's black motorcycle boot with a silver ring on its side, protruding from beneath a black tarp.

It was a trip he asked me along for. I declined. I was nineteen; I'd just been accepted at Berkeley. I had a new boyfriend. A party to attend.

In the wrongful death suit, his life was valued at fifteen thousand dollars. Exactly enough to pay for four years of tuition.

What did you do, Dad?

I declined to go to Redding, I declined obliteration. I missed an exit you took. I could have gone quickly, gone young, gone with Gayle, who was ebullient, who was my friend. I could have missed all of this.

You invited me, and I said, *Not now.* And so instead, you gaily embarked. You paid for college, sending cash down from the sky. A rain of guilt, a rain of love.

You died viewing wreckage. You died with the love of your life. In heaven, Shakespeare clapped. How I miss your style.

You died with your third and most beloved wife Gayle. You died not on the same year or the same day, but in the same instant. Your spirits climbed entwined.

A pact, my mother said.

She cried for weeks. I didn't understand. Weren't they divorced? Hadn't they gone to court?

I went to class. I drank. I broke up with a kind man and found a worse man. I had two abortions within nine months. One for my father and one for Gayle. I was trying to replace them, to carry them back to me, new.

Good intentions, dressed in black.

I didn't see my father's body when he died. He died madly in love and an alcoholic, the kind that never goes for help. The Neptune Society burned him up. It was the seventies; funerals had gone out of style in California. I don't know exactly when the Neptune Society did it, but I know they did. It was like when bulky-refuse day comes. It just comes; they haul whenever they get around to it. And anything you would have like to save or retrieve out of the trash, anything you might have wanted back, an old footstool or a standing ashtray? It's gone.

I found his journal in the flat, on the one day I was allowed in. Red leather, a blank book filled with his handwriting. I found his Malcom X glasses, bent to the shape of his elegant head. The tobacco tin where he kept our pictures and tiny hospital bracelets. Girl, Finnamore. Boy, Finnamore.

I found, in short, everything.

The Jumping Clock

"When your father died, I knew because the clock jumped off the wall," Bunny once told me. We were sitting in her brightly colored kitchen, where all truths and revelations were served.

"No, it did not," I said.

"Yes, mija. It did," Bunny said.

Beat. Sip of tea. My mother likes it with heavy cream and honey. My mother's tea is more like an ice cream sundae.

49

"And then the phone rang with the news," she said.

"For a long time, I thought it happened in the reverse order. That the phone in the kitchen rang, and I knocked the wall clock down as I picked up the receiver."

The yellow wall phone. She had it removed not long after that, I realize.

"But it didn't happen that way," she said. "Richard never could wait to tell me things…when you were born, I woke up in Recovery. And I looked up, and here he comes running to me in scrubs, crying, "She's here!!""

We sat in the glow of this.

Why are men always leaving? I remember thinking. *Where, I wonder, are they constantly going? And there is this: Once they get there, why don't they stay?*

"I don't know," Bunny said, as though I'd spoken aloud.

My Real Mother

I need to see her once more. A special daughter dispensation.

No way, says the sky.

Why am I writing this? Why am I trying to spin gold out of straw? What am I hoping to accomplish?

This is happening to my mother, and to me, is the *leitmotif*. I am dying, I am finished, my kind is at an end. But so, what?

Clinical depression is standing at my door, caressing the jamb. I run harder, a Red Queen.

In the face of any trouble, my mother used to say, *It can all be fixed.*

This all can be fixed.

Magical words I will never hear again. The sound of her laugh on my voicemail, a lost symphony.

I go away alone to the ocean to write. All night, there's a mystery sound in my hotel room, close by and intermittent. I think it's a foghorn, but it is still there in full sun the next day. Soon, it's all I hear. When I am not hearing it, I am waiting to hear it.

A man comes from engineering, his face open. I describe the sound, which has disappeared. We wait in silence. A not-uncomfortable silence. Suddenly, his eyes look up.

"I hear it," he says.

I change rooms with gratitude. I am not insane.

An invisible hand reaches out to me from Dementia. Later, a slim finger from husband and child. I fear something will happen while my back is turned, black shoes always poised in the air. Death has followed me to Santa Cruz.

I think again how depression really does feel like you are in a slight depression in the earth, serving some sort of time. You don't see what others see. You don't see what you see.

I have been here before, but this has lasted a long time. Its roots lie in my mother, my country of origin. They are bone and viscera deep.

These are heavy bricks I'm laying down, one by one. The more I lay down, the more I unburden myself. The more I lay down, the more I see are there.

You can avoid falling in love. You can avoid getting married or having children. You can avoid friends and distance yourself. You can come from a laboratory, know no father. But you are not free.

Everyone has a mother. Everyone is eligible for loss.

When This Happened

We don't know when this happened. We can't say *It was 8:28 when the plane hit the tower*, or *That was the day everything changed*. Our trauma as a family, if there is any, is not vectored to a single point. We will look back late at night and say *When was it? How could I have missed the signs?* The indigo sky will laugh. It too has no inception date. It always was.

In the country of Dementia, Time is not recognized; its onset is mired in imprecision. This is nothing like an execution. No. One day an invisible mist, an intrepid poison with a long, tangled fuse, a gossamer swath of disorder simply dropped from thin air to swath my mother. The binding spell complete, she turned back from where she was headed and began her long journey back to source. Where she will again be whole. The ancestors she talks to on the ceiling...? She will join them. Fly away.

Save Yourself

I had the intruder nightmare again. In the dream, I hear scrabbling sounds from the other room while I am on the phone trying to dial for help, and I can't get through. The phone won't work. When I look at it, it's cracked, and I can't remember how it happened. Then the scratching noises begin again at the bedroom door, and I wake up shouting *NO*.

"The message is *No Escape*," Augusten says.

"Really?" I say.

This seems excessive. Where are the protective forces of Good?

"Divine intervention is bullshit," he says, with his trick of reading my mind. "We get to save ourselves."

There are times in caretaking my mother when I think about the relief it would be to simply not wake up in the morning. There are moments I'd prefer to not exist. Yet suicide is not an option. Not for me and not for my mom. Also, Augusten has forbidden it.

If you did that, within five years, your son would be dead. Suicide passes through families as surely as a virus. He would absolutely have overdosed by thirty. You need to just STOP.

I too believe suicide is just like a virus. Besides that, the women of my family don't kill themselves. If anything, they soak up the lifeblood of others and live to be 104. That's the Puerto Rican way.

The Necklace

Once when he was on book tour, Augusten signed a book for someone who complimented his necklace, a jade disk on a leather cord. When they walked away, he ran after them and gave it to them, slipping it off his neck.

"Wear this. It will keep you safe."

This exemplifies who he is. A gifted writer, certainly. But primarily a healer. A shifter of fates. When he got out of rehab and shared some of the stories with me, I said, *You should write a memoir about this and call it* Dry. It's now part of the curriculum at rehab facilities.

I ask him if he remembers the necklace incident.

"I do remember running after the person and giving them my necklace. They had complimented me on it when I signed their book.

"I sensed something in the person, a need for connection, perhaps…something that I couldn't begin to fix, of course.

But I could do something to make sure they knew I truly heard them and that I saw them: I could make an extreme gesture, so they would know they were special."

When he was writing *Toil and Trouble*, he made me a magic wand out of hickory wood, a wand he carved over water, in a boat, in keeping with tradition. His arms were covered with scratches from the tree's thorns. He polished it smooth, wrapping silver wire around it to hold gemstones. At its tip is a silver cap. Tonight, the moon is full. I wave it overhead and point it toward the sky. I say the best prayer I know, via Anne Lamott. *Please, please, please. Thank you, thank you, thank you.*

Therapist

I'm not sleeping. My doctor doesn't hold with sleeping pills. He suggests talk therapy. I spend twenty minutes on Zoom with a therapist I find on the Cigna site, Claudia. A free consultation.

Claudia is my age, brown-gray hair, Midwest accent, wire-rimmed glasses. I give her the one-minute synopsis of what's happening right now. I have been practicing this; I can flip a switch and recite it at will. I needn't feel.

"First of all, I am so sorry for your loss," she says.

"Thank you."

"How are you faring?"

I am a boat headed out to sea. I can feel myself heading out there, day by day.

"Not great…"

I pause. Every word costs me something I can't afford.

"I just feel so hopeless and tired."

"Are you having suicidal ideations?" she asks.

Claudia is not fooled by my one-minute recitation of *The Daughter is Fine*.

"Sometimes..." I say.

"Do you have a plan?" she asks, but casually. *Do I have a match?*

"I would never do it," I say.

This is true.

I don't want to die; I just want to skip forward and no longer watch my mother lose her mind and body. Late at night, skyscrapers, speeding trains, pills, and cliffs dance before my eyes with the silken allure of Scheherazade, suggesting a way out. Telling me stories, a hundred an hour, all about ways to disappear, to be delivered onto a distant shore, clean, shriven. Away from Dementia. Away from all incipient loss. Suicidal ideations are tropical islands I can visit and return from.

"What you're feeling is normal. I don't see how you could avoid depression, frankly. What else is going on?" Claudia asks.

She wants more. She knows there is more.

"My grown son lives far away..."

She nods. A small, apologetic smile.

"You just spelled out a formula for having a hard time, Suzanne."

"Mmmmm," I say.

Nodding, not speaking. Fatigue is pulling at my bones.

"The dark night of the soul," Claudia says.

"Dark black," I say.

"I should imagine. Yes."

"I feel I should be doing better."

"You shouldn't. It's a mistake to try," she says.

"It is?"

I take a deep breath. I feel like I've laid down a bundle of hay, while on my back is a hay baler going full blast, ridden by a fat man with a hat.

"I feel like I'm drifting away, but toward what? I don't know."

"The drifting piece is important," she says. "You don't want to grab onto something just to keep yourself from drifting."

"Okay," I say, thinking of the desired sleeping pills. The ones that, *oh just by the way*, cause dementia.

"This is an opportunity for old stuff that hasn't gotten the tending that it might need…" she says.

Other dead people will be covered, I assume she means.

We set a date for our first weekly session. I resolve to continue for as long as I can manage. Yet I suspect my insurance will not cover anything this good and will try to snatch it away.

Broken Clouds

Externally, I function. I take care of two households, scrubbing four toilets and three showers and two ovens. I pre-treat stains and fold a world of laundry. I graze on small bits of food; it matters not as long as it is bite-sized and bland. I talk to Pablo, to my friends and family.

I slip, and I feel myself slipping.

Down I slide, quietly and with dazed incomprehension. A part of me—the youthful part, the part that felt lucky and immortal and free—is dying, crumpling, and curling back into myself like the Wicked Witch of the East's pointy striped shoes, after the house has fallen on her.

And now illness is a clear and present danger for me personally. Disease came for Bunny, and then it U-turned back around to wave and say *You're next*.

As I look at my phone, I see local weather is calling for Broken Clouds, and I think, *Exactly.* Then I drive to McDonald's for a Happy Meal. It's just what I want.

I am losing hope is the feeling that wells up from the bottom of my feet to the tips of my hair follicles.

I look around my house for something to do, to take me away, but I have dwelled too long and am mired here for now. Maudlin self-pity engulfs me. Rivers of this shit run through Dementia.

Tom walks into the room, looks at my face. I think he is going to say everything will be all right. My baby-bird mouth is open.

"I couldn't do what you do," he says.

I realize I am using none of the cleansing and healing psychic tools I learned in the nineties at the Berkeley Psychic Institute, what I think of as *Witch School.* We learned how to read tarot and ground ourselves. I was thirty then, neither wed nor a mother; no one was dying or ill.

Now those tools seem quaint, like children's toys. I can't help noting that new-age spirituality was the first thing my mother abandoned when her mind broke.

Proviso

There may not be a jolly ending to this story. Heidi is probably not going to fling off her crutches and run toward Grandfather.

Brujeria Tips from Bunny

It's almost Halloween. The magic trend is amusing to those of us whose mothers, grandmothers, and great-grandmothers have been household bruja for centuries. From when I was very small, I understood the power of words and intention. And hair.

Recently, I found a small, heart-shaped tin of human hair at Bunny's house. I am working up the nerve to ask Ron whose it is.

It's not mine or Pablo's—of course, I checked. I am thinking Grandma Sarah.

Yes. Grandma turns her head for a picture, and Bunny quickly takes small scissors and snatches some hair, thinking, I am sure, "This hair will be instrumental for a spell at a later time."

Bunny always takes hair from each ancestor; it is part of her program. If catastrophe happens and should she need a miracle, well, Bunny has the hair.

"Always clean out your brush," Bunny told me when I was young. "Wipe the bathtub behind you. Empty the drain and clean it, mija. Don't leave your garbage where anyone can get it. Even a lipstick stain can be enough...just one tissue...or soaked nail files in a pinch..." she finishes thoughtfully.

"What if I want to get rid of someone?" I asked.

"You write their name on a piece of paper."

Mira, she said, reaching for a blank envelope, what I will come to refer to later in my mind as The Envelope of Death.

"You write their name down. First middle last if you have it. Then you erase it."

"What do I do with the envelope?" I asked.

"Mail it as soon as you can."

"To who?"

"Mail it as soon as you can," Bunny repeats. "Use it to mail a bill."

Presumably, we don't care what kind of nefarious voodoo runoff comes to AT&T.

A Note from The Universe

To: suzannefinnamore@gmail.com
From: TUT Notes From The Universe
Subject: Note from the Universe, Monday May 31

Time out! Time out!

What do you mean, Suzanne, you can't see it? You don't know? You aren't sure?

You're scared?

This is an adventure; you're an adventurer, uncertainty, fear, and even setbacks happen. Besides, "easy" has never been your style, and just because you can't see the miracles doesn't mean they aren't happening, doesn't mean you're alone, and doesn't mean you're on the wrong path.

The day your ship arrives, and it now swiftly approaches, the confusion, fear, and setbacks will be among your fondest memories.

Today, Suzanne, you're exactly where you most need to be—
The Universe

Did I subscribe to this while I was stoned? I may have.

I hit Reply.

Dear Universe: SCREW you

In other news, my phone informs me that my screen time is eighteen hours a day, up 276 percent. I do a social media cleanse. After a few days, people are concerned.

"You deactivated, so I wanted to check in…"

I assure them I am fine and just taking a short break. They assume it is because of grief, but it's not: it's envy and anxiety.

I have to deactivate twice, once on Facebook, and once on Instagram, which I know is just another way crazy people can touch me, but I love the filters.

This is what I won't have to see any more:

> Brenda Townsend Browne: Hiiii! Can you guess where my Mom and I are on vacation?? #nofilters #Cabo #grateful
> (Picture of ecstatic silver-haired woman and daughter at sunset, smiling and clinking balloon wine glasses.)

You would be surprised at how little I want to accompany you on a guided tour of your next trip to the Loire Valley, Brenda. You would be surprised at how people like me resent people exactly like you even though we sometimes hit the Like button, or even the Love button.

There needs to be a Jealousy button and, furthermore, a Bitterness button. When that comes, I'll reactivate.

Baby Rabbit

When my husband Tom mows the lawn, he never does it all the way. He'll always leave a patch of wildflowers somewhere. In North Carolina at my little house, he liked using an old push mower that someone had discarded on the side of the road. He cleaned it. He sharpened its blades. He knew how.

One spring, a rabbit began a cursory nest on the front lawn. Tom was mowing, and he spotted it, very low to the ground. He piled up leaves and sticks around it to make the nest better. Safer. A few days later, he reached in and pulled out a baby bunny.

Has Draymond Green fouled out?
Was it a flagrant or a common foul?

This is the Warriors' last time out, so the question is vital. ESPN switches to Steve Javie, a retired referee speaking from his living room, explaining that since the contact was above the shoulders, it is a flagrant foul.

The color commentator Reggie Miller agrees, the tallest thinnest brown man alive, with endearing jug ears. He held the three-point shooting record until Stephen Curry snatched it away.

Things are decided instantly and for all time in basketball. Bodies crash through the air, slide across the court without breaking, and I know each one. Their strengths and weaknesses and free throw average is at my fingertips. None of them will die, but some will lose. There is nothing to fear here.

I heat up some refried beans with extra cheese and splat on some sour cream and watch the Warriors and yell at the TV. I curse and throw my arms up in the air in triumph when a clutch play happens. I do things in front of the basketball game that I don't do anywhere else. It's incredibly freeing.

It feels as though I have been writing and mourning Bunny forever, but this forty-eight-minute game is just starting, and beautiful, athletic young men will fly through the air like giant magical elves.

Over the years, I've gotten into the NBA deep enough, so I can be interested in every game, not just the Warriors's, both statistically and in the moment. That's eighty-two games a season times thirty teams. It's a massive, sweeping wall of distraction. The thrill of a Warriors win doesn't last the way it does when you have a baby. But I am here, and they are here.

It's their final season in Oakland before they move to San Francisco, and like my mother, they are in Transition. There is nothing to be done but marvel at the beauty of the magnificent flying elves and their spherical leather orb. When the regular season ends, I will watch the NBA Draft. I will watch the Summer League and then the Pre-Season games until the regular season begins again. I will faithfully abide.

Pegao

Today, I am wondering why my mother used hamburger grease in her arroz con pollo recipe, which was astonishingly good. I want to call her and ask her but cannot. I would also like to consult her on *pegao.*

Pegao is the Spanish word for the crunchy, delicious rice bits that stick to the bottom of the pot. This crust of rice is a delicacy. Once the rice is served, the *pegao* is scraped out and distributed as a treat.

When they were children in New York, Bunny and Pinkie used to fight over who got the *pegao* that stuck to the bottom of the caldero after Abuelita had made arroz con pollo. And so, I was taught to achieve the perfect crust—caramelized and crunchy, but not actually burnt, scraping the bottom of pan with a wooden spoon, making sure to dislodge any stuck bits. I was instructed to cook my rice over very low heat and try to refrain from lifting the lid, enabling the perfect *pegao* to form. At the end, you flip it in a dramatic fashion, ensuring that you get double layers of *pegao.* This takes courage and bravado in equal parts.

Our people shun electric rice cookers. They are thieves of *pegao.*

Later, I see my uncle at my parent's house. He is still droll and has lost another inch, as he seemingly does every year. He moves low to the ground at a surprising clip.

"Why are you named Pinkie?" I ask. I already know, but I need the story again.

"Well, we were pretty poor," Pinkie says, his eyes not leaving his phone as he cross checks the eBay inventory of his store. "And the neighbor had an extra layette, but their baby was a girl, and so everything was pink. And I got it."

Pinkie is eighty-two and well. Pablo has a theory of why Pinkie has lived so long, outlasting every man in our family by decades. My son believes that the Puerto Rican god has a list of names and that the god saw Pinkie and thought Pinkie was a girl, and so he was spared by a clerical error.

The Question Man

There was an ongoing human-interest column in the newspaper when I was growing up. My parents were featured at the very top one day.

DEC 23, 1974 SF CHRONICLE

The QUESTION MAN
By O'Hara

WHATS YOUR IDEA OF A SEXY GIFT?

Bunny Mathews, public school secretary, 2ⁿᵈ Street, Oakland.
A vibrator. That's a real sexy gift, I think. Those leopard bikini shorts for men are sexy. I've seen them in Playboy, *and they look terrific. They advertise some pretty sexy underwear in* Playboy. *Satin sheets would be good, too. Blue satin sheets to match his*

65

eyes. I think fur feet pillows sound good. I got that from Playboy, *too. It sounds like all I do is read* Playboy, *doesn't it?*

Ron Mathews, printer. Jordan Rd, Oakland

Last year I bought Bunny some sexy lingerie. Lace pajamas. They were pink lace, and you could see through them. Pink lace with pink satin trimming. It really looked nice. I got them too small, and she couldn't get all the way into them, but they still looked good. Satin sheets are a good gift. Satin sheets are very sexy. I've been looking at that ad for satin sheets for a long time. I might go for them.

I was in high school when this ran in the newspaper. My mortification was absolute. But now I appreciate it, and recently, I took the clipping home from their house. Their photos in the paper are faded almost to nothing. But my mom is laughing, and she has a perky black beret on her head. I can see that. They are happy together. They fit.

I like the idea of the Question Man roaming the streets and wish he still did…maybe dressed in a white suit with black shoes and a beret. I have a lot of questions that maybe he could find answers for. *When will this end? How will this end? Am I doing enough? Who was my biological grandmother, what did she look like, what did she do with her life? Where did she live? How many more children did she have? How was my mother conceived—was it in love or lust? Why did she never come back into our lives?*

I tried Ancestry.com. Nothing.

If an island woman doesn't want to be found, there is no help for it. She will make the water close around her.

What Love Is

"It's our fiftieth anniversary today, and it means nothing," Ron texts me.

"What can I do?" I asked.

This is the only good response to anything that happens here. Not *Why* or *When*, or *You've Got to Be Kidding*, or *This Makes Me Want to Scream*, but *What Can I Do?*

A gift of coquito was decided upon, to be delivered in a quart mason jar. His favorite. And my mother's, once upon a time.

Still, he goes on loving her every day and night, sleeping by her side and monitoring her medication and nutrition. This is what love is, not a feeling deep in your chest, not a sunset kiss on the beach, not a diamond ring or 3.2 million followers on Instagram. It feels as though I am watching a toddler repeatedly lift a cow overhead.

Angry Young Men

Pablo isn't responding to my texts. For two days. The text score is Mom 12, Pablo 0.

I have long since stopped trying to leave a message; his voicemail isn't set up. That's how they all are now. Millions of young men, parachuting straight in from high schools in the sky. The angry young men with iPhones. iPhones their parents pay for and track them with. Except, now Pablo has turned his Location off. They all do.

Pablo is taking life a bit haphazardly. He moves soulfully and moodily with occasional wildly creative bursts. No worse than I did at his age, if I examine my records, but still. I expected him to be different. Instead, he's a mirror, not just of me, of certain qualities of Mark.

I imagine him mugged, face down in a pool of his own vomit. I think of his body sprawled beneath a freeway overpass; his cranium smashed in by an aggressive transient. He could be at a seedy hotel *filled* with bedbugs, about to be knifed and flung out the window.

The score is now Mom 26, Pablo 0.

He's ghosting me. I've a ghost son as well as a ghost mother now. It's a relief to see a pattern to the fatal attachments.

I have lost control of my son. Of everything. Anything could happen to him, and I won't be there. I won't even know. A phone call from the police. A doorbell in the night. Then blackness. Nothing.

Why is this happening? I have a box of Oblique Strategies cards by Brian Eno, a kind of Bible dipping I do when the mind fucking becomes too rowdy.

I choose a card: *Abandon Desire*

Big sigh. Abandon the need to understand why things happen. Abandon the need to know what is next. It might as well say, Abandon everything. It might as well say, Be a dog.

"That's right," Augusten says, when I tell him. "That's the gold standard."

Empty Nest

What I primarily remember is how comforting it was to occasionally sleep with Pablo in his little boy's room, how even though it was a twin bed, we both fit fine. It made no sense, but the bed seemed plenty big for us both until he was about four years old. Maybe five. It happened less and less, and then one night was the last night.

Sometimes, I would watch late night TV and walk downstairs, meaning to go to my room but not making it there. Going to Pablo's room instead, with the blue night light, that one blue lightbulb in his floor lamp that stayed lit throughout the night while the two white bulbs were dark. Being drawn by his faint boy scent. He never woke up. We would breathe in time, another unlikely thing. We would take a deep breath, and both turn over on our sides at the same time, like two halves of a seashell. Sometimes at 3 a.m. he would wander into my bedroom, sleep walking, and get into my big bed. I can't remember the last time.

He's twenty-three now. He's twenty-two miles away, and he is a thousand light years away.

Jesus Christ, I say to the air.

How can this have happened? I was never going to be like my mother, who would call me at college and say, "Last night I dreamt you were little again..." with a maudlin, wistful expression.

I text Mark. *When will this be normal?*

Together—are we together? For the first time in a long time, maybe we are—we sit with it.

Brief Encounter

This morning, I see my doctor, who looks exactly like Barney Rubble on the *Flintstones*, for a brief Check In visit. He is older, and he doesn't wear a fur toga, but basically, it's Barney Rubble, right down to the booming laugh and the small, beady black eyes. I have to come to his office in Lafayette in person every two months so he can refill my small Saint Joseph Children's Aspirin dosage of Xanax and my Prozac gummies. We meet every sixty days, even if I haven't changed one single thing in my life or diet, even if I feel exactly the same. I used to see my doctor once a year, but now that I am medicated, it's become an ongoing series of twenty-minute visits.

He asks the same questions; I give the same answers. Apparently, he must check and see if I have a screw coming out of the side of my head or look for evidence of children's blood splashed on my clothes. I don't know what it's about, but I suspect it's about money. I walk away with the Xanax prescription clasped in my fist. I practically run to the drug store. I know this is problematic, but I feel I need every available crutch as I watch my mother disappear.

Gold

New Year's Day. I visit Mom; she is in the new multifunction adjustable bed that is set up in the living room in front of the giant flatscreen TV. There are two XL Twin identical beds, side by side, with separate controls. I crawl onto the other one, where my stepfather Ron sleeps. He leaves for the grocery store. I am here, so he can leave.

Bunny is not pleased, but Ron pushes back.

"Suz is here; I will be back in an hour."

And unexpectedly, I see her smile. I see that some of what she does is for show.

She turns her shoulders toward me in a confiding way and asks, "What's new, Tudes?"

A good day, after all.

She has many names for me. As a child, I was Suzie, then Tootie, then Tootie-Poo, then Tudes for short. The names, it seems, can never get too short or far away from what we are born with. I have an uncle named Pinkie, after all.

I tell her the novel I wrote last year has been rejected by twenty-one editors, many of whom didn't bother with even a form rejection letter.

She asks me what the book was about. I tell her the plot, very slowly and carefully, of a ghost story. She's not tracking; she looks troubled. I change the subject, but not over much.

"Mom, when you die, do you think you see everyone you've ever known?"

"I hope not," she says, with a look of physical disgust.

We laugh.

Not everyone can visit Dementia. Those who don't will never find the gold doubloons hidden there.

Richard Comes Through

Today I sync my phone to my laptop and receive a grid of black and white photos of me with my father, when I was two, for no reason. Thirty-six reproductions of the same picture, even though my software is set against importing duplicates. Even though this photo is not on my phone, or it shouldn't be. And why today? I haven't seen it in years.

It's one of my favorite pictures of us together. It *is* my favorite. I see Dad wearing his buttoned-up shirt and khakis and his Buddy Holly glasses with clip-on sunshades as we stand in the backyard of Abuelita's house. I see that my hair has been butchered by one of Bunny's home haircuts, and I am wearing a diaper and holding what? A hot dog? Eating happily, no shirt on, completely relaxed. I see my father's wedding ring. He will repurpose it twice.

When I was young, I called someone "dead to me" as a matter of form. "He's dead to me." I didn't know what I was talking about; I didn't know that by saying this, I was actually summoning. I didn't know about the way the dead come lurching to life.

Let Nothing Go

I have to get my teeth cleaned this morning; I forgot to cancel. The pointy sticks, the hooked device, the X-rays, and the icy water jets. It's what I deserve, clearly. I go every four months, so my gums won't bleed out. I go in an effort to reverse time inside my mouth, which, like the rest of me, is aging in a violent manner.

The theory of my dentist, and in fact all dentists, seems to be, *I need to harm you, so you can be better. I need to file your teeth down to bloody nubs, so they can be whole again.* I am on a strict regime, and so every four months, we all join hands and go through the Looking Glass. My dentist is talking implants, so that he can retire young. Implants on all of the molars, what he calls the *Load Bearers.*

What I secretly believe is that I don't need every one of my molars. I can lose both the first and second, which I am right on track to do. It's a genetic flaw: my father had short roots on his teeth, and so do I. I won't live to be 120; I can slide the fuck by on the teeth I have. My mother's teeth are fine. It's the gringo teeth that have betrayed me. Every time I mention my frequent trips to the dentists, my Uncle Pinkie looks very smug, very nifty. He has all his teeth. He lets nothing go.

I don't tell my dentist about my mom. When he asks me what is new, I say *Oh, nothing*. I treasure these people on the periphery of my life, the ones I don't have to tell.

The Haircut

All Ron has is big, dull scissors. They suffice. This is not a salon. This is a war.

I crop her white hair to the scalp, particularly in the back where it will mat from reclining day and night. I tell her we are getting matching hair styles. I leave some bangs.

It comes out strangely well.

"A beauty queen," Ron says, kissing her forehead. Lifting the cow overhead once more.

My mother's hair always grew straight up and out, so any attempt at length was always thwarted. Any attempt to prune the Rican hair only makes it grow back twice as thick and coarse. But she worked with it. She frosted her hair, just a piece in the front and two wings at the side.

She had a leopard print jumpsuit that she put on after work. For evening wear, she had purple sequin disco ball earrings with a three-inch drop. A low-cut wrap dress in zebra.

She had flats. Lots of flats. A short woman, she did not attempt height; she stayed low to the ground. The better to spring.

Irony

Another five hours at my mom's house. It helps me as much as it helps them to be the capable one, the youngest person in the room. To be simply a daughter. The time for being a daughter is limited.

Mom is getting smaller and smaller. She has eaten the wrong cake in Wonderland. She was heavy for most of her life. Now she gets to be thin but can no longer walk. It's so Monkey's Paw.

Each visit, I fear my mother won't recognize me. This will erase me. She'll pick up an Etch A Sketch and shake it, and I'll disappear.

I announce myself loudly.

Hi Mommy. I love you!

She sits and stares at *America's Got Talent* and *The Voice*. Sometimes the Nature Channel. Sleeping many hours a day, her slack jaw is a hole.

It takes so much energy to pull her away from where she is. Often, I don't know if I should. If I have the right, or if it is right.

The Patient Lifter stands in the corner, a medieval device. A metal contraption that lifts my mother and carries her to the other bedroom while she cries out in alarm. The affordable male nurse.

I hate the Patient Lifter. I need the Patient Lifter.

I want her to go into the hospital for a week so that I can transform their mobile home into a showcase. Or at least take everything away and clean underneath. I want her to go to a hospital and drift away peacefully on morphine.

Why am I not more evolved? I should not be feeling; I am the well one.

The Patient Lifter looks on knowingly and with great patience.

Unanchored

Pablo is still gone. Bunny is still dying. I feel unanchored. I also feel abandoned. I don't need Augusten to explain this to me, but I text him anyway.

Augusten isn't playing.

"This is just the beginning of the loss. Pablo is a very special young man. You've done an amazing job."

Thank you, I say. I preen in his praise.

"He will have a career God knows where. Fall in love. Where will he live? Texas? India? NYC? He'll have kids of his own. You'll never get enough time with him again"

This is refreshing. I am not hearing any of that They Come Back to You nonsense. As if children rematerialized in their bedrooms wearing jammies, fully grown with giant whiskey lollipops.

"Well, he was ready to go," I say. "I had become an impediment to his trajectory. He was starting to look at me like I was a meter maid, and he had one-minute left."

"He does have one minute left. He has to individuate," Augusten says.

I sigh heavily.

In some ways, I feel like I've already had enough time with Pablo, good and peaceful and uncomplicated time, and it seems wholly right that he has his own place and his own life now. I don't need him to be the emotional center of my life; that's my job. His job is to grow up and leave.

And he has done that.

"FUCK," I say.

"CONGRATULATIONS," Augusten says.

Funhouse Mirrors

Today I enter the house as Ron is wiping my mother, which makes her furious. She is shouting insults. Peabo Bryson is singing *Tonight I Celebrate My Love* while pictures of the dead cascade across the giant TV. For just a moment, I can't believe this is true, but it is.

"I want it to be over now. I want her to be at peace," I say to Claudia that evening.

She nods. "That's normal."

"I'm having to follow her into a very dark place," I say.

"Without a light…" Claudia adds.

In all the ways that matter, my mother is gone. But she is still alive. That's confusing. It's crazy-making. When I am there, I am performing, acting like she is okay, acting like I am okay, trying to get her to respond, which compels me to do things that are insane. It defines the word *senseless*. I must join her in her country to communicate.

Dementia sucks you in with a terrible centrifugal force. It puts you in the position of wishing your own mother dead. Sometimes yourself. You begin to not be able to separate, you live in a funhouse-mirror reality. It seems infinite. All you know is it will run downhill as the brain is corroded. It's not like cancer where you get treatment plans and a timeline. It's far more nuanced.

How do you deal? If you're my brother, you deal by disappearing.

Often, I no longer think of my brother as missing something vital and precious, as being deeply mistaken. Sometimes I think of him as clever, avoiding this country and its downward slope altogether. He may, I consider, be wise. A fucking sage.

"She's stuck," Claudia says. "But you're stuck too."
I book an extra session.

Welcome

Another birthday. I am grateful but wary.
Getting old means invisibility and a flattening of events.
You realize you won't go from triumph to triumph in your life,
that it's someone else's turn now.
I am sixty-three and feel eighty-three.
Welcome to Dementia, where even if you don't live here,
you will feel as though you do.

How To Fall

"How did you and Dad fall in love?" Pablo asks while he is visiting from Asheville.

"How does anyone fall in love? You fall...you don't stumble, you don't glide, you don't sally. You fall, and you fall hard. It's the easiest thing you can imagine. It involves no effort and you can't plan for it. Falling out of love? Completely impossible unless pushed. There is the one who pushes, and the one who is pushed," I say.

I must have had this speech prepared for a long time.

He nods.

"When I met your father..." I tell him over a grilled cheese sandwich I am making for him, sliding in some pickle slices, "...the conditions were exactly right. We met, we fell in love, we had a baby, and little by little, he fell out of love."

I place his sandwich on a plate. It's too hot to eat now. There is a period of consideration.

"We were both in. And then he pushed me out," I say.

Pablo looks at me with skepticism and a kind of horror.

"It's normal," I say. "It's fine."

"It doesn't *sound* fine."

"It's like walking into a room full of flowers. You walk in. There are the flowers. One day you walk in, and the flowers are gone. It's not gradual. But sometimes there's a child you can never stop loving. And that love makes the other love look paltry. You say you will never do that again. And then you go right out and fall again."

"Hmmmmm," Pablo says.

"What if you don't know right away?" he asks. "I meet a lot of girls I think I could love. Almost every day. I'm on Tinder."

"If you don't fall," I say, "if you don't have the actual sensation of falling? It's not love. Also? if you fall before you meet them? That's not love either. That's fiction."

"Oh. Good…" he says, imagining the fall and not being able to get out of it. Imagining being pushed.

Pablo has always liked to be in control. He did a swift combat crawl until he was ten months, then he stood up and walked almost perfectly. He hated his stroller because he had to be strapped in.

"You favor your father," I say. "You will be fine. I predict that you will always be the one who pushes."

Pablo smiles.

And I can practically hear Mark *cackling*.

"When I die," I tell Pablo in the car on the way to the airport, "I want them to play *When The Music's Over* by The Doors, the album version, not the live version. There should be a celebration and food *there* already, so people can start stress eating at once. Nothing maudlin or grotesque."

"I'll take care of it," Pablo says.

He gets out of the car and walks toward the gates. Just as I think he isn't going to, he turns and waves.

Vorverlust Gefühl

I feel heavy. I wake up and need to cry but can't. Because nothing has actually happened. My mother is still alive.

Instead, I cry watching the Olympics, and during an astrology reading, and at Chapter Eleven in *The Accidental Tourist*, when Macon Leary says

> *The first year was like a bad dream, but the second year is real.*

I find reasons to cry that aren't about my mother. All the while, the pressure quietly builds. To be released some day in the mythical future when this is over.

Anticipatory grief is dense and has no focal point, a dust storm. Each day, it coats me anew.

On a bad day, Bunny asks to die, to have Ron kill her.

She does not do this in my presence. That is a *yet*.

I see the Germans have a special word for the long goodbye: *Vorverlust Gefühl*. A feeling of anticipatory loss.

I listen to it on the translation site. It's a long, silken word, like the sound of someone falling through pillows for several floors, landing softly.

FORRRRFELLLLLLUSSSSTTTEPHOOOL

I listen to it over and over as though to integrate its mystery. As though if I understand something in German, I will understand it my life and avoid it altogether, stepping nimbly by its harm.

Mortality Bingo

Today, as I zoomed with Claudia, my head grew very heavy. I propped it with my hand and tried to look deep but not catatonic. Earlier, I had set up my vanity light, which has an arm to hold my phone and another, higher arm with a circular beauty light on its end. If I just hold the phone in front of my face, I look like a sad pudding.

She asked if I kept a journal. I said I didn't, but I document everything in some elliptical way because I am a writer. She didn't ask me what I write. She didn't say *genre*. I mentally issued her 1,000 bonus points.

She wanted backstory. I laid out the facts of my life like squares in the game of mortality bingo. Dead people, live people. People in between.

Loss. Loss. Ambiguous loss. And here? My son. Gain. My friends. Gain. My husband, who I can lean on. Gain.

I don't know how to grieve the living.

"I've hit a wall," I tell Claudia.

I talk about the dust storm of anticipatory grief and how uncertainty reigns, how I wake up and feel dread fall on me like a blow. And because this isn't a place in which I want to stay, I keep going, moving forward as a way of being. The writing and the cooking and the running are my practice, though I'm struggling to believe in something new right now.

"It's fresh air," Claudia says, "out of the dust storm."

Now the dust storm is real in the same way that the country of Dementia is real.

"It can hurt," she says of the dust. "It can sting."

"It's lonely," I say. "Tom isn't in it."

"And maybe scary," she says.

I tell her how Tom said I couldn't save my parents or protect my grown son—and how this was news to me. It was *news*. I tell her how all of this feels endless, though I know that eventually things change.

"Your husband is your constant. You have a constant role as a wife," she says.

This feels like a radical statement. What would Gloria Steinem say?

I tell her I'm grieving my son. *The child is gone*, I tell Claudia. I explain it to her.

"What did you expect?" she asks.

"I expected that I would miss him, but I didn't expect pain. What do you tell other people?" I ask.

I want a prescription. I want to outsource this.

You've done such a good job, she says brightly. *Time for you to fly now, and re-focus.*

"But what if I don't feel like flying? What if I am old and heavy?"

A zeppelin versus a glider. An elephant versus a gazelle.

"It will happen slowly," she says.

I want to cry but am conscious of a need to not tarry here. We still have five minutes.

I grope for good news. I tell her about my recent Pap smear, where they found abnormal cells, and I thought I had cancer. But the next tests showed I didn't.

We cheer.

"Now you have a dust storm!" she says.

Black humor is my friend. Without it, no one survives this country.

Emojis

Those Facebook emojis of a little face hugging itself with a heart trouble me. They seem like pity dressed up as love, emojis sent from the land of the sane, the land of folks whose parents are either fine or are ensconced in expensive facilities. There is a secret bitter space between me and the emoji givers, between me and the place Eudora Welty designated as *Where your mother keeps her cow shit.*

I am so not evolved.

My mother is where she is supposed to be, I tell myself. But is she? Might she be getting better care elsewhere, had we the opportunity?

I've been posting a lot of pictures I've found of our early lives together. I have been breaking the news of her demise and acting as though everything is fine. I scroll through my news feed, where the healthy and the able-bodied parade, where I see hale octogenarians hiking and celebrating birthdays in restaurants. Baking bread and sunbathing and posting their Wordle scores.

I have no business on social media right now.

Once more, I will shutter my account for a few weeks. I will keep away the pity of strangers which I, myself, invited. I will hang tin in my trees to keep tweets away. In the South, they hang bird frighteners, homemade reflectors made of rounds of tin.

I don't see why this had to happen to her. To me. It's so unfair. And as I think this, I hear God chortling. *Where were you when I made the world?*

The Bath

My nemesis The Patient Lifter has been called up to transport my mother to her former bedroom. Its canvas pouch is unhooked, tightly rolled up and placed next to her. We rock her once, twice, six times. Unroll it in stages and center her on it. Lower the machine. Hook the pouch in its grooves. Pull the manual lever. She rides in it like an unhappy float. She loathes all change.

While she is on the other bed, we change her sheets. The several protective pads. I run warm water and a magical foaming solution over several soft cloths.

"Why are you doing this?"

"Leave me alone!"

Her body is her land, and we are trespassing.

"Why do you hate me?"

We tell her she needs tidying. We tell her she is loved, and this is why this is happening. What she feels is a lie, we tell her. Another lie.

She looks at us, glares and bares her teeth. She has done a spell of transformation: an animal.

Ron wipes between her legs. A valley, a no man's land.

I position myself at her head, place my fingers on her forehead, caressing her in an upward motion. I croon; I wash her hair with warm Wet Wipes, one at a time, surreptitious. She shuts her eyes. I take a deep breath. She takes a deep breath. The animal recedes.

"Always use an upward motion," she said at her vanity mirror in 1970, applying Ponds Cold Cream. She was a movie star then, but the animal was inside. Waiting. We all have one.

When it's over, she is clean. We transfer her back to her bed. We give her a mango smoothie in a sippy cup with a bendy straw. She smiles.

I think of bathing the dead. A silent, sacred ritual without the animal. But this is the living; this is who we have. She is our baby, not small and new but twisted, ancient. A relic being tended.

There is sacred, and there is *sacred*.

A Drastic Turn

We go away, one week.

"Your mother has taken a drastic turn for the worse," Ron texts me, while we are in a boat on the ocean.

"Who hasn't?" I involuntarily think. "Who won't?"

Then I panic and begin calling United. By evening, she has stabilized.

My mother, my main person, has been dying for years as her brain shrinks to the size of a lace doily. Dying slowly and uncertainly, with huge dips in countenance.

Come Armageddon come, as Morrissey sings.

It seems we pay for every really good thing we get. We pay in heartbreak. I get that, especially in an election year. And things come in waves. My mother will die, someone else will die. I can see Abuelita waiting in the clouds, hands clasped in lap, an apron neatly tied at her waist.

Endings come, her solid body says. *One goes on.*

Land on the right side of an ending, good. You survived. You prevailed. Land on the wrong side, there is work to do.

Right now, there's a compelling dramatic tension between the two political parties, a distraction from my own personal array of loss and incremental gain. I enjoy watching CNN and seeing the rats flee down the ropes, away from the listing luxury liner with white life preservers. I'm enjoying it in the same way that I enjoyed the film by James Cameron.

In short, the air is moving quickly and seemingly in the right direction, but it's tense and pressurized. Everything can end either well or badly at any moment.

I lie down. I turn off CNN, which I have had on twenty-four seven because I'm afraid that if I turn it off, the bad things will get worse.

The Letter

Claudia says that I should write a letter to my mom, telling her what she has missed.

Dear Mom,

Here is what you've missed since you moved to Dementia:

COVID-19
Trump
The insurrection
The California fire seasons, including 2020 where the sky turned red like Mars
The War in the Ukraine
TikTok
Elon Musk
Kanye West
Monkeypox

It may be that all who wander in Dementia are not lost but simply biding their time and skipping over the unnecessary bits.

Reentry

Back from our trip, I visit right away, though my urge is to avoid. And it's a bad visit, the kind that crushes souls. Reentry deals psychic bends. The whole next day, I stay in bed after an energy spiral.

The moment you cross into Dementia, vacation ends. And the country is getting so dark. Daily, the path narrows. I want to stop time so as to not lose the few memories of my mother, whole, which are being corroded by this. But no, the factories here stay open all night and must do their implacable harm.

The cost of living in Oakland is egregious, and we will move when this is over. But I suspect my mother is a witch who will live forever. She seems to defy gravity and live on avocados and chocolate milk. A river that needs nothing but its rage. Her life force even in repose is astonishing.

I want to see it through to the end but not experience it. I want to be a good daughter, but my selfishness is shining through, a kind of survivalism. Fantasies of her assisted suicide twirl around the edges of my mind; something painless and instantaneous and surrounded by scented candles and loved ones. They dance away when I realize I don't live in Scandinavia. How many other daughters are going through this right now? I want to stand in a field with them, holding torches. I want to dance with them in white robes.

I know what Bunny would say if she were in her right mind, which is that I never have to visit again, not even once. But where is she? Not dead, not alive. *Ni de aquí, ni de allá.* Replaced by a stranger with just glimpses of her former self.

A woman of keen intelligence, my mother always said she wanted to be smothered with a pillow if she became senile and her mind went. But when she said that, she had a red bandana on her head, and she and her brother Pinkie were laughing; Ronald Reagan was president. And what about criminal charges?

Everything leads to something worse if you try to intervene with what is.

I text Dee, saying I am cratering emotionally.

No bueno, she says, and suggests a gummy.

In fifty years, we have gone from sneaking a smoke and swilling Boone's Strawberry Hill behind the 20 Building to CBD gummies. A glamour surrounds childhood friends; we can be young and old as we like.

This is the filling station on my way to the next stop in this country.

Garbagebar

My friend Ken and his boyfriend Niki took the garbage-strewn backyard at their San Francisco Middle Haight building and made it into a beautiful garden. Ken took all the trash and debris the slumlord threw in the yard and made it into an outdoor bar and oasis, using old cabinets and pieces of marble countertops and fireplaces. They excavated every stone and planted a lush garden. They recycled a child's puppet theater and made that into a dark shrine covered in soft green moss and filled with crystals. A variety of herbs and succulent plants are laden in rows on cinder blocks and freshly painted boards. They rolled in an aluminum cattle trough and piped in water and silent electric feeding pumps and filters and added fat orange koi and white koi and mosquito eaters. They trained jasmine in long lines to the sky, creating vertical space.

There is a whole area under the rickety death trap back stairs that is enclosed and has a complete bar with glassware. They put in midcentury modern bird feeders and a small labyrinth that I walk on in tiny steps. We named it GARBAGEBAR, and I had little cards printed up that say *GARBAGEBAR. Happy Hour All Day.* Ken had matchbooks made that say *I Got Trashed At GARBAGEBAR.*

Without San Francisco and without Ken, I feel like I might veer off course to a bitter land. They are in my sanity tool kit.

Ken was forced to rush back from holiday to San Francisco last Thanksgiving, when the koi pond rebellion happened in the dead of night in his backyard. It was an attempted coup, where the raccoons tried to eat the fish and take over Garbagebar.

Raccoons are an ongoing problem at Garbagebar, but the squirrels are fed daily from ceramic plates with squirrels on them, and sometimes this is filmed and posted on Instagram, where Ken has many followers who wait for the squirrel feedings. He has named the squirrel bar Risu en, which means "squirrel park" in Japanese. He and Niki have named each squirrel. *Paco Fandango. Boo Boo Squirrel.* There is Ryan Fluffington, and his mother Arianna, who are part of a dynasty founded by a big old red squirrel named Duke Fluffington, who hasn't been seen this season and is presumed kidnapped. The Earl of Huntington Falls lives in from the self-named island of Golden Gate Park, and his street name is Earl the Squirrel. When Ken walks in the park, squirrels run to him.

"Can you just stay there permanently?" I ask Ken on the phone today, when he talks about the allure of Healdsburg. "You must never leave."

"Well, technically I will never leave," Ken says. "I have rent control; even if I move to France, I will never technically leave."

Tonight, I will go to his fantastic Queen Anne Victorian flat, where we will drink Aperol spritzes and thwart the attentions of the raccoons, who will dance away while they plot their resurgence. We will laugh when there is no reason to laugh. We will make a way out of no way.

The Stranger

I go to my parent's house.

"Who is she?" my mother asks Ron.

"It's me, Mom."

"It's me."

The incantation has failed.

She shakes her head and looks away at the large flatscreen. Three men who met in a school cafeteria are singing *Fix You*.

I begin to scrub the kitchen floor.

My mother is agitated. I hurry, cleaning faster, headscarf ablaze, a parody of my entire family, all of whom were maids at one point, as was I. I begin at the corners and work my way inward.

"I want her out of here NOW!"

On my knees, I am shouting an apology to my mother as I scrape food from the floor. There is a bag of old onions in the butcher block cart rack, soft and dripping brown goo.

I'd been relentlessly cheerful and helpful for these last few years. I see now I was expecting some reward. That someday she would turn to me, whole. Hand me the key to something.

As I leave, I tell her I love her, sending the words over her head. A white flag.

Cleaning

At fifteen, I made six dollars an hour cleaning houses. I walked to my job after school in the hills of Oakland where I was bussed to attend a nice, tree-lined high school. The people of color were released among the affluent. Everyone sorted themselves out. It was a festive mix, all teenage misfits beneath the skin. Some rich, some poor, and some like me, in the clingy middle.

I cleaned for a kind, subdued woman who had white wall-to-wall carpet and central vacuum cleaning. You placed a white tube in a hole in the wall and the suction happened. Money made this happen, enabled this woman to hire me and go shopping in the Tony Village of Montclair. Money meant freedom and magic; I saw. Once she left, I ate food from her refrigerator, quickly. Never enough to be missed, just parts of things. Afterward, she paid me, and I walked down to the flatlands where we lived.

Sometimes, I still dream I am walking home down Redwood Road. It's summer, and I can feel the pitch of the hot cement beneath my shoes. Where the road curves and the sidewalk ends, I can feel myself clinging to the dirt shoulder, leaning my whole body away from the speeding cars. After a long while, the sidewalk begins again, and I can walk straight. I know it's a long way, and I know I will make it.

Ghosts

I read ghost stories and tales of disasters. A passenger on the Lusitania saw her exact double and was almost instantly struck dead. Her companion said that seeing that woman, so like to the other, was a harbinger of doom. Moments later, the torpedo struck.

I think of how my mom started writing her emails in all caps, sending my birthday cards to the wrong address. Why didn't I know?

Doom is exactly where we are, is in fact a major city of Dementia. But we are also still in life. There is nowhere to go, not for her, legless and tongue-tied, bound to her bed and unable to walk, like a sea creature washed ashore. Like an enchanted queen damned by a jealous witch, doomed to live the same day again and again.

And there is nowhere to go for me, who moved back to be with her. Here we are.

Doom is a place my brother is hesitant to visit. A man who never gave up his dreams, never asked permission. Someone I never see, though we occupy the same city. A kind of ghost.

For everyone who travels to Dementia, there are a thousand who cannot.

Falling

I don't know how to tell Ron that seeing my mother like this sometimes plunges me into despair. That to see this progress and deepen is shattering on a psychic level.

Of course, he knows.

This is the year I have had to give up the idea of myself as a wonderful daughter, impervious, protean. I was flying at that level for a while, ascending and gyrating, busily improving what I could in Dementia. But then the atmosphere thinned, and I fell.

Patti Davis, who lost her father Ronald Reagan to Alzheimer's, says that you won't be the same person after losing someone this way. I can already see that she is right. But who am I now? Which I am I?

Time, the great destroyer and healer, will let me know. When I hit the ground. When she dies.

As I write those words, I betray her. As I continue to live in the world where she no longer roams, I betray her. None of this is true, and all of this is true.

My mother taught me that the crone is the goddess of wisdom. Marion Zimmer Bradley writes beautifully of this in *The Mists of Avalon*, a book she introduced me to. One of the many books she pressed on me that we read together and referenced in conversation.

My mother has forgotten how to read or write. So yes. Old age. Transitions and loss. The watching of things as they move away. The question of faith.

I can see that as I go deeper into the country, I need to ascend or be sucked into the vortex of despair, a persistent weather pattern of Dementia. I need to rise up and get clear on what is. This is the Crone's aerie, above what seems to be.

TWO

What Was Found

In a Wonderland they lie,
Dreaming as the days go by,
Dreaming as the summers die:

Ever drifting down the stream—
Lingering in the golden gleam—
Life, what is it but a dream?

Lewis Carroll

Rings

This morning, I bring my mom another ring, a tremendously gaudy fake pearl. She loves it. The urge for jewelry never dies apparently. She is serene, bare faced, her untamed hair a white nimbus, her brown eyes unadorned: a crown free of its plain muslin wrapping.

Endlessly agile and cunning, Bunny slides back to childhood in New York, calling her husband of fifty years *Daddy*, gliding forward to her first marriage to my father, touching down only briefly in the Now, where she is admiring her ring.

Rings are of great value in Dementia as they can dazzle and are never out of reach. Standards of fashion here are relaxed, along with the pretense of monogamy. My late father rises in Dementia, and Bunny asks for him to me.

"Where's Richard?"

"Dad's not here right now, Mom. But he's fine…"

Visitors to Dementia know that everyone is fine, no matter how long they have been dead. There's a wonderful economy of souls happening here, where no one dies and all are comrades on the road. I'm pleased to speak of my father in the present tense. It's like visiting a house you lived in and walking around, just remembering.

For a while, I explained who was alive and who was dead to my mother, but ultimately, it dragged down conversation. Now I've given up control. I go along, and everyone is alive or dead depending on the moment, a much finer system. And who knows? It may be that my mother knows the way things really work.

I am my mother's memory now, its curator. I point to the Parade of Faces that prompts her. I tell her who I am; I tell her who Tom is. I tell her who her grandson is. There's a moment of blankness. Then the spark. She remembers. We are making fire.

Spells

I have a small wooden magic wand I wave over my mother and myself and Ron when things get too grim. It lights up at the tip and makes a whooshing sound. I found it on Fourth Street in Berkeley, just seven dollars. I picked one up and pointed it at the cashier and pushed the button. She was visibly alarmed. I bought two.

I gave one to my mother, who was always a witch on Halloween. She used it with some help. Now it's too difficult for her; her hands don't work. Now I must cast spells for both of us.

She doesn't remember anything about those Halloweens. The last five decades are erased, and the previous three are in motion, sliding away from her visage. A telescope in reverse.

I have Sarah's old black painted maracas from Puerto Rico. On my mother's birthday, I shake them as I sing the song. She looks at me with wonder and faint derision. What does a birthday mean to her, she who is beyond time, who can be in Central Park in 1944 or The Summer of Love in San Francisco, as the mood strikes? What matters this, to a citizen of the wind.

When I ask her if she remembers New York, she smiles. A stoned look comes over her face. She's not on narcotics, and so I know she is remembering. We sit together and think of New York, its majesty and its people. Dementia has no dominion here.

Bunny-isms

Today, I compiled a small list of things my mother often said so I won't forget.

On Dating:

Is he Jewish? Jewish men are great.
Well, for God's sake, don't sleep with him.
Have you heard from He Who Must Be Obeyed yet? Oh, you'll hear from him. He's like the tide—it comes in; it goes out.
Are you burning your candle at both ends again? Just don't go crazy on him. Come from the heart.

Whatever you do, don't tell him about _____
(recent scandal).
Your father used to do that. Drove me crazy.
You have to kiss a lot of frogs, Suz.
Until you see rings, you don't owe him a
thing. Nada.
The treasure doesn't do the hunting.
Just be yourself. Don't start prancing around.
How did he like your apartment? Was it clean?
We have to get the Man Trap ready.
What did you wear? Wear classic styles.
You should join a cooking class. That's the
mother lode.

Malapropisms

Why should he buy the milk when he's got the cow?
You only live thousands of times.

On the Spiritual Life

You know what you know.
We shall see what we shall see.
Thoughts are things.
A client called today and said I had been almost
100 percent accurate and thanked me for helping her out. I don't remember a single thing I
said. I just check out.
You shouldn't have said that. The spirits
heard you.
Just ask for the best for all concerned. That's
the formula.

Earth is the insane asylum of the universe.
They still burn witches, you know.

Pools of Light

There are pools of light at my parents' house. The little fountain
on the side of the walkway where Pablo used to hunt snails. My
mother's class photograph from Van Nuys High School. The
books of mine I find with articles tucked inside. The very first
poems I ever wrote with loopy, lacy spirograph illustrations, for
my mother. The crystals on the porch I bring home to clean: a
giant pink quartz and a gaggle of raw amethyst. Everything I
bring home is something our children will throw away.

I push this thought away and find another pool of light in
the laundry room where a large troll doll stands with orange
hair, daring me not to smile. The troll is surrounded by several
smaller trolls, all glue-gunned to the top of the bulletin board.
The troll has a tribe, and the tribe stands beside him.

My mother glue-gunned everything down so that her
clients who came for Tarot readings wouldn't steal things.
Remembering this is another pool of light.

Whammy Dust

I secured a medical marijuana card at once when Pablo moved
away. There are no witnesses now; I can do anything. I am
heavy into something called Whammy Dust and have gained
nine pounds.

In other news, all quiet on the Dementia front for three
whole days. It may be that THC keeps harm away. If so, bring it.

Still here. I breathe. Take another hit. Time passes. Every single second, I think, people are born, live, and die. The giant celestial bellows of the universe just breathing in and OUT.

Still alone. More alone, in fact, after the Whammy Dust than before.

It occurs to me that maybe my life isn't a reality I particularly want to heighten right now. I vow to throttle back on the Whammy Dust.

And I do. I switch to just a daily eighteen-to-one CBD to THC ratio pill in vegan capsule form. A tiny coconut oil buzz and simultaneous calm. A smoothness to the body. I feel just slightly lubricated. *I wonder if the Native Americans knew about this?* I think as I spray a little CBD on my tongue.

You Are Here

We are in COVID-19 lockdown. Month three. I wear two masks to my parents'. I don't want to appear as the Angel of Death.

My mother hates the masks and reaches to tear them from my face.

I just said to my husband, *I am tired of you. You sit in one place, and the world revolves around you.*

I whisper, though.

Of course, I am describing my mother and also myself. Will this lockdown never end?

Whispering ridiculous things to Tom from another room when he can't hear me is how I vent my spleen and ease the strain of constant togetherness in our small house.

I want to get on a plane, but there are none. The world is now a small dot with the words *You Are Fucking Here.*

When he drives to Oroville to go fishing, I am gleeful for one day. Then night falls, and I begin to panic. When I call him, he answers at once, like 911. Tethering me back to earth.

Every Saturday, he cooks a whole pound of bacon, perfectly and slowly and with great care. He will stack the strips on a foundation of paper towels and spread them out just so, layering them, forming a papery fragrant bacon house, which historically is the centerpiece of his bacon sandwich apparatus. Sunday is French toast with bacon, always made with sweet Hawaiian rolls and cardamom and real maple syrup.

When the kids were young, we would all line up and make our custom BLTs. Pablo liked his with avocado and a whole egg and a splash of Valentina's hot sauce, which we bought by the case. His was a BLEAT. Both Tom and Pablo have Valentina's Hot Sauce scarcity issues.

Once the world acknowledged that pigs were intelligent, many wouldn't eat pork. But we are overlooking this because Tom and Pablo love it and because all the Ricans have long ago made a fetish and a religion out of eating every kind of pork that could be maimed from the ground beneath their little hoofs. They worship at the shrine of *pernil* and *lechon*. Roasting a whole pig is not out of the question for any festive event.

Tom worked as a breakfast cook at Perkins Pancakes during college, and the habit has never left him. He rarely cooks less than a pound of bacon and a sack of fried potatoes; there is always extra toast. His eggs are always perfect, basted or fried or scrambled soft.

"Pigs are smart," Tom says. "But bacon has no brains."

The Proposal

Christmas, 2009. We are in the kitchen at the little house in Old North Durham with my son and Tom's two children. Faye is seven and is laughing. Nash is eighteen months and trundling about with authority, knocking things off surfaces with an even, majestic sweep of his arm.

Faye asks Tom if we are going to get married.

He turns to me.

"You have to ask," I say.

This isn't happening, I think.

He takes a knee on the old linoleum.

We eat Costco Christmas cookies. I find champagne flutes and a bottle of Prosecco. Pablo and Nash have a snowball fight; in the pictures, you just see a blur. Magic won't travel through a lens.

We'd known each other five weeks.

What does this prove? The irrelevance of time. The sovereign nature of clarity. How when you know a melon is ripe, it's ripe.

Twelve years ago, today. Also yesterday, tomorrow. The good things, the things that last, never stop happening. Something my mother knows where she is.

That first Christmas, a plain brown box arrived with a vintage plastic life-sized baby Jesus, hollow. There is place inside for a small pink light bulb, his sacred General Electric heart. It came to my house directly from eBay. No receipt, no note. A friend? My mother? No one claimed it. Sometimes I think that it came from the place where the impossible waits to be born.

Wishful Psychosis

I can hear my mother's voice in my head now that she's almost all the way gone. A tête-à-tête. A private conversation between two people.

Wishful psychosis is what Freud would call this. Except I don't exactly wish for it—it just happens. So, just plain psychosis then.

Normal is what my Puerto Rican family would call it. Like hearing an echo in an echo chamber. The most natural thing ever. And I know it's her. She is just the same as ever, if not more so.

She tells me not to stop dying my hair. She tells me not to diet. She tells me not to use eye cream because it's nonsense. Spend that money on books, she says. She tells me everything I don't want to hear but, in all truth, probably need to hear.

"You can't go back and you can't go forward. There's only now," Bunny says.

The loss of a loved one marks you somehow. You feel chosen, or almost chosen, the brush of something large and dark. Death has familiarized itself with you and your surroundings. There's a sense of suspense, a black shoe hovering in the air. You want to go with them. You want to lie down as well.

I can just about get to the store and the doctor and my desk, but that is all. Terror strikes at the sight of any large vehicle approaching. I no longer assume it does not exist to mow me down. It used not to be like that. It dates from her diagnosis. I just aim for things in the middle of the road, defying them not to destroy me.

Loss is not quite the right word, nor is abandonment. It is not only to do with being left behind but with something that happened, something momentous and terrible and Lord of the Rings-y, which finds its echo in this world. This is why so much a glimpse of her sunglasses, no longer in her possession, create such a cosmic pang I can feel it on this side of the divide I've constructed against all of this. "Anticipatory Grief" is not adequate to describe the significance of what is happening— just as "Apparition of the Virgin Mary" or "Little Green Men" are inadequate to describe otherworldly phenomena. Self-help authors try and cut it down to size, but it's not cut-able. It just is, like a slow-moving glacier. We must allow the glacier.

Another Perfect German Word

> *Verschlimmbesserung* (Ger.): Supposed improvement that makes things worse
>
> *verschlimmbessern*, To make worse by "improving."

I can see that trying to make things better for my mother—A new blanket! A new music tape! More chocolate!—is only moving things in the opposite direction. She gets overwhelmed. She gets indigestion. She gets angry. I resolve to try to do more by doing less.

I think of what Bunny would say about that. *Don't push the river*, she would say. An apt saying, as it's easy to see how you can't push a river. If you try, not only will you fail; you will be swept away.

Dr. Barney Rubble

Dr. Barney Rubble retired, so I have stopped taking the half a milligram of Xanax I was taking at night to sleep. But due to the generosity of Dr. Barney Rubble, I still have a bottle of sixty tranquilizers. So, I can only have sixty really bad things happen to me.

Xanax depresses the central nervous system, and I am tired of begging for them. Now that Dr. Barney Rubble has retired, this is a perfect end point.

I see my new doctor today—a woman—and will tell her the Xanax is out of my system (it only takes twenty-four hours). It's a huge relief. But I also feel junk sick. So, I was a junkie.

Still taking the Prozac, as without it I fall into depression. I have to take it for a while longer, maybe the rest of my life. Zero side effects on that. I still get one Sonata every fifth night, for sleeping. But I was boosting it with a baby Xanax, and so now I am wide awake.

I will be wide awake for a couple of nights because this is the peak withdrawal time. I am looking forward to dreaming again. Because Xanax sort of stops that. It stops libido, too. And—hi ho!—it can lead to Alzheimer's, and I don't want to go there before I go there. I have to parachute straight into my life without a parachute. It's honorable but also hateful. I liked the Vaseline smear that covered my lens. But that's all over now.

Dolls

In her sixties, Bunny started collecting dolls and stuffed animals at yard sales and dressing them in tiny clothes, placing them in wooden highchairs and itty-bitty rocking chairs. Rabbits and teddy bears were a theme, but she would take anything and make a family out of it, make an imaginary being out of it; first a small group in the corner of the bedroom and then branching out into the living room. A teddy bear in spectacles and overalls. Two identical bunnies with long brown ears and red tartan sweaters.

Did she talk to them, call them her babies? If she did, I blocked it out.

She was roughly *my age.*

I don't have dolls, but I do keep my son's stuffed rabbit on my desk. Its stitched black eyes are looking at me right now. Once again, I see life as the big surprise party you insist you don't want but which happens anyway.

FaceTime

Saturday morning, I FaceTime with Ron. We talk about the wet leaves in the roof gutters and how they need to be dry before Tom can come and eradicate them. We talk about my Uncle Pinkie, who has Parkinson's but whose medication is working, and so he doesn't shake. His brain is still fine. In the candy-based game of life, Pinkie got the red Chuckle, and Mom got the black Chuckle.

Mom is eating her bananas and scrambled eggs. When Ron holds the phone in front of her, she sees me and motions for me to come closer. Closer. As if I can walk through the phone and hand her another banana.

I tell her I love her. She says she loves me too. This is our one act play; we repeat it daily. Like *Phantom of the Opera*, the show goes on for years and is always somehow fresh to us both.

She is there, and I catch her eye, and then she is gone, turning back to her piece of toast. The aperture to her brain opening and closing, opening and closing. I think of the windmill hole at the miniature golf park. As always, I wait and hit the ball when it has a chance of going in.

Bullshit Oranges

Just now, I hear the *choo choo* alert sound on my phone that means Pablo is calling. Yay, I think, and snatch up the phone, readying myself for the mommy-joy infusion.

"Where are you?" I say.

"Trader Joe's," he says. I hear the whir of the shopping cart and the voices of busy shoppers.

Pablo has always enjoyed grocery shopping; he sees it as a form of eating. He explains to me about oranges. He breaks down clementines, tangelos, mandarins, Cuties, navels, and something called Cara Cara. Volcanic oranges, from the sound of it.

"Those are the big pink oranges in a special display kiosk at Trader Joe's...I passed them by and was confused..." I say.

Pablo vouches for the Cara Cara.

"You open them up, and it's good inside..." Pablo says.

"There are a lot of bullshit oranges," he adds with something like real disgust.

I write down BULLSHIT ORANGES on my phone and think again that without Mark, none of this would be possible.

Eaten by the Chupacabra

We can't find Tabby, the declawed orange cat that isn't ours. She was irritating me the last time I saw her by very aggressively cleaning herself and making repetitive smacking sounds. Now I feel bereft. I want her back. I keep going to the window and calling her and whistling the mindless short tune I'd devised for her.

She arrived not long after we moved here, and I named her—a mistake. Once you feed something, you can still get away, but name something, and it's yours. Name something, and you cross an invisible threshold, and you can't cross back. You can't tell the cat to leave, and you can't control the cat or divorce yourself from the charm of the cat, and so loss becomes a possibility. An inevitability, I see now.

That cat came along, and she tricked me. Now she is off tricking someone else, or worse.

I miss her. I miss the particular scent of her clean white paws, which were foreshortened by the owner who'd declawed her. They smelled like grass and baby leeks that grow in the grass. I also called her Short Paws because a declawed cat is a cat whose digits have been shorn off at the first knuckle. One of her ears was split just very slightly. I liked the things that were wrong with her, all of her scars. I liked thinking how I would have prevented them.

I even miss the little parts of dead birds she would deposit at my feet. The tiny sparrow head. The ruffled torso of a wren. She was evil, but she gave her gifts to me.

Today is day eight and no cat. I freshen her water bowl. I take the bag of Iams dry food, and I shake it, a mnemonic device.

Nothing.

But there is still an opportunity for a grand reunion, a surprise treat where—just as I have stopped looking for her—she will slip around a yard corner and call for me. I will, late at night, hear the sound of the cat door opening and shutting, that flat thwapping sound where the rubber edge of the hinged door meets the magnet. I will see her crooked face.

I am waiting for that sound. It is not coming. This feels hideously symbolic. I can't hold on to anything. Everything passes from me.

I go to the window again and open it again. I scan the horizon.

Suz, that cat was never yours to begin with, Bunny says in my head. I sit down at my desk. Pick up the Fisher-Price Chatter Phone. It's time for one of my secret Lifeline Calls to the Bunny of Old. I talk to her, and I imagine what she would say back, and in fact, it is exactly like talking to her in 2005. The connection is clearer and clearer the deeper she moves into Dementia.

Hi, Mom, it's me.

Hi, Tutti, she says. My nickname.

She has questions.

What is the cat's full name?

Tabby.

My mother waits. She waits to extract more information from me. She always knows when there is more.

Her other name is Short Paws, I say. *Sometimes I also call her Queen Neferkitty.*

Hmmmmmmmmm.

I wait. I close my eyes, and I can hear the sound of my mother's tiny Sony in the kitchen where her Telenovela show *María la del Barrio* is playing. A woman is crying, and a man is laughing derisively as the music swells.

Yes, it does feel like Queen Neferkitty may be on the other side, Bunny finally says.

But how? If she were hit by a car, I would have heard or seen something. I have driven around and put up signs, Mami, I say.

*She'll be back. Probably. Although...perhaps she was eaten by the chupacabra...*Bunny muses.

To Bunny, this is what happens to anything that has disappeared that she cannot explain. A lost cat? A missing glove? A wayward boyfriend, last seen walking away from his pickup

truck toward a taco stand? Eaten by the chupacabra: a mythical goat-sucking creature first sighted in Puerto Rico in 1995.
It sucks the blood of mostly goats, but all small animals are
in peril. It is described as Big Foot with teeth. Bunny believed
in the Chupacabra. She appreciated the way it was born on
the island and then went on to cross cultures. First appearing
in Puerto Rico and then Chile, China, Thailand, Russia, the
Philippines, and North America, including a rash of sightings
recently in Texas and some in Florida. She felt that, much like
JLo, the chupacabra best represented her adventurous spirit of
joie de vivre.

*I l*ove you Mommy, I say. *I miss you terribly.*

I am right here, always, Bunny says. *Where else would I be?*

Boomerang

I tell Claudia that Pablo was laid off due to COVID, which
throws me into feelings of incipient doom. His bad news makes
me feel anxiety, guilt, and pity. I am a black belt codependent.
He has money in the bank; it's not the money. I need to know
where he is, and when he had a fulltime job, I knew. Now he's
out there, all loose.

"Learn to accept the feeling but don't hold on to it. Accept
it, and say I'll see you later," Claudia says. "He's twenty-three.
You need more practice in treating him like an adult."

"You're riding the wave," she says, and smiles.

I doodle a hundred tiny bubbles on my notepad. There's
something jolly about Claudia. No matter how I feel, I see her
on my phone, and my mood lifts.

She asks how my mother is. We wonder what this time is doing for me. How it teaches compassion but also exposes limits to which attention must be paid.

For the first year or two, I waved off these emotions, saying that Ron had it worse, as did Bunny herself. I waved the psychic harm away, but it boomeranged back.

I know now there is nowhere to hide and possibly no reason to hide. As Robert De Niro says in *Good Fellas*, "It's what it is."

So Many Restless Legs

Granddaddy Purple cannabis strain is recommended for my midnight mad pony dance, the restless legs syndrome that has gotten inexplicably worse since I moved back to California. I buy some low-THC gummies mixed with CBD from Mountain Remedy because they have free delivery and the best gift bags. Today, the gift bag was an edible sample. I chew a peach gummy. And I am completely OOB.

Checking my email on my phone, I see that Clean Wine has come to Thrive Market. Exclamation point. There is also a Primal Kitchen at Thrive Market. "NEW items you've GOT to try! LOAD UP ON everything from avocado-oil mayo to collagen peptides."

I am mildly intrigued by collagen peptides but resent the fact that I have *got* to try them. One of my earliest memories is my mother saying, "I don't have to do anything but die." So, I may not open this email either.

Every morning, I wake up and shovel email into Junk, and I furiously Unsubscribe. I must click on them one at a time, they never come in groups. They come singly, assassins of both my time and whatever peace of mind I've somehow cobbled together during the night. My eyes read the subject line on their own accord. Another, separate fishhook. I unsubscribe to *Mother Jones*, *Patagonia*, *Goldberry*, and *Trout Unlimited*. It does no good. The imperatives to *attend* grow in the night. They cluster around my inbox, each muscling forward to claim my emotional poker chips.

This morning, there is Clean Wine and Thrive Market. I want to know more, though I also know it's ridiculous and wrong. I sense something has gone too far here in California and perhaps the United States as a whole. We appear to be going both left and right and forward and backward all at the same moment, creating a kind of shock. A state of chaos. It must be so for something like Clean Wine to be celebrated and claimed as real. And for a place called Thrive Market to exist that actually only exists on the internet. Essentially, there *is* no Thrive Market. It's a mirage that happens to ship wine from warehouses in Fresno.

The fact of Clean Wine troubles me. Have I been drinking bad, dirty wine all along? Are the nutrition police coming for wine as well as food? They are. They are here at the digital door, banging to get in and make things right. It's insidious and more than a bit frightening. The Nazis more or less invented organic farming. The maniacal zeal of the fanatic runs both ways.

I want to be neither Left or Right but in the real life, non-Thrive Market *middle*, but I've noticed it is very hard to stay in the middle. It's like trying to balance a scale. I will continue to try.

The Oakland Gardenia Social Club

"The twenty-sixth meeting of the Gardenia Social Club will come to order..." Dee says, doing a high kick in the center of Jack London Square in front of the Oakland Pier. As she does this, a tall, stately Black man with mirrored sunglasses walks by and gives her an appraising look.

"Robert?" she says.

"Dee. How you doing?" he says.

"*Quite* well," she replies.

We all four check him out. He is magnificent.

Dee walks away after wishing him and his wife blessings. We scuttle after her.

"He's cute!" I say. What am I, twelve?

"He's full of bullshit," she says warmly, and we continue onward toward Kincaid's.

We have the gardenias for our hair; we have the bobby pins. Me. Dee. Diane Green, whose name is now Naa. Lisa Stark, who is still Lisa, but her last name has changed twice. Lisa beat colon cancer and learned to ride a motorcycle with her boyfriend, Marques, who also went to high school with us. It's ninety-seven degrees, and all four of us are wearing the biggest hats we own along with custom hand fans. We take about a thousand pictures. There will be craft cocktails, and the words *I HAVE TO SPEAK MY TRUTH* will ring forth. That is the mantra of the Oakland Gardenia Social Club. After this mantra is said, many scathing truths ring forth.

"I have never liked my brother. When he calls, I let it go to voicemail."

"Why is Ayesha Curry everywhere now? I look around, and she's everywhere."

"I miss Andre Iguodala already. I'm kind of sick about it."

"They better retire his jersey."

"I wonder what a mini face lift would do for me. But I am a coward. Also, broke."

We all nod. More bread dripping with garlic butter and tarragon is placed before us. We fall on it.

"Trump is going to win again. Landslide."

"All the same people will vote for him. Our side is scattered."

"Republicans be organized as fuck."

"I love to just sleep. Nothing else touches me the way that does."

We all agree that melatonin laughs in our faces. What we need are the hard drugs, the kind no doctor will prescribe any longer.

"I miss your mom," I say to Naa.

Chloe, who was always Mrs. Green to us.

"We all do," Lisa says, signaling for more ice water. "I'd come to your mom crying, and she'd say, 'Baby the sun always finds a way to shine behind the clouds. You keep looking for the sunshine.'"

We clink glasses. We order another round.

These truths are like small freedom flags planted in our lives. We'll meet again next year, leave a large tip, and stay for hours. They know us at Kincaid's. They see us coming, four women of a certain age with gardenias and a swaying walk. No one can stop us.

Air Dementia

Claudia asks me if I have a fear of flying, and I say, *No, I have a fear of not flying; I have a fear of stasis. I am never so comfortable or serene as when a plane is taking off.* It seems the truest thing I've said in therapy. A cornerstone. My biggest fear, in fact, is being stranded in an airport in an unfamiliar place, being trapped on the tarmac for a long time. That's where I am with my mom. On a tarmac in Dementia, waiting to take off for a better place. The seats recline into a bed. The pilot is God. The movie is the movie of our lives. The cocktail cart is rumbling down the aisle with chocolate milk and coquito. We are trying to make the best of it.

The plane is full of people like us. There are half a million more, idling just behind. Our numbers are legion. We wait, and while we wait, we sing songs of childhood, eyes up.

Morning Rituals

I wake up early. I emerge from sleep's kind blank page, the clear open window into oblivion. I remember freshly the fact of my mother's hospice, and I feel glad. They finally approved her for hospice based on her decline. We are no longer on our own.

Then free-floating worry and stress lands on my head, the tsunami of current losses and secondary losses and the losses to come. The gates of anxiety Hell yawn wide for me, as the incessant mind chatter and litany of worries and the lists of things to do begin to play in my head like a mad polka. What Anne Lamott calls Station KFKD, station K-Fucked.

But I have a system. I take a Hydroxyzine, which is essentially a decongestant, to melt the edges of my anxiety. I cross-addicted to Hydroxyzine after I went off Xanax. I breathe. I turn on my *I Dream of Jeannie* diffuser, which is shaped exactly like the bottle Jeannie lived in. I check the water level and refill the lavender essential oils that Claudia suggested to relieve stress. I put it on a three-hour timer. The tiny circular holes in the Jeannie bottle diffuser are softly lit with alternating color lights. Blue. Pink. Red. Orange. Green. The colors project into our small bedroom.

I open my Audible library. I listen to Anne Lamott's *Halleluiah Anyway* and *Help, Thanks, Wow*. I listen to Eckhart Tolle's *Essential Meditations*, or his lecture *The Path to Liberation from the Pain-Body*. And while I listen, I play Toon Blast on my phone I am now on Level 5,329. When I run out of lives on that, I switch to Toy Blast. Level 5,699. I keep my hands busy so they don't reach for the unknown. When I rise, I do laundry and haul down our winter clothes from the attic.

As my mother edges toward the lip of oblivion, I try to stay organized because I know when she dies, there will be so much to do—most of it grieving. I clean out my Inbox; I clean out my closets and the garage. I try, unsuccessfully, to stay off my phone and social media because it propels me in so many directions. I feel myself lurching this way and that, a tiny shell in an eddy of ocean. But something is alive inside.

Remembering

Today, I go to Bunny's house and steal back all my first editions because I'm running low.

I sit with my mom, who is like a Buddha now. I listen for metaphysical gems.

Bunny calls her husband of fifty years "Daddy." Then she slips back into place. It's like watching a mobile. Mostly, she is happy. And when I show up, she says, "Can I get you anything? Something to drink. Or eat?" She forgets that she hasn't been able to walk in three years.

My mother was always filled with optimism. You would never catch Bunny whining. My father left her, and Bunny was devastated, but she also squared her shoulders and was, like, "OKAY *FINE*" and went back to work and took care of business.

My mother went to something called Parents Without Partners when my dad left in 1967; it was sort of like online dating in its infancy. She met a man named Bill Kinsel who really liked her and took us all to see *Snow White and the Seven Dwarfs* at the Grand Lake Theatre in Oakland. I can't believe I can remember his name. But she wouldn't sleep with Bill Kinsel, so The End. Then she met Ron at her job.

This sort of memory thing drives people I have grown up with crazy but can come in very handy. They will wonder, *Who was the homeroom teacher who always had mended clothes?* "That was Mrs. Holmes," I'll say. "She would raise her arm, and there would be a safety pin holding her sleeve on. She lived in Walnut Creek but worked in Oakland."

Who was the scary math teacher at Bret Harte in eighth grade?

"That was Mr. Wade," I'll say. "He had yellow fingernails and was clearly a raging alcoholic. Tom Hanks had his class and did a spot-on impersonation of him lurching toward you with his pointer stick."

What was Tom Hanks like in high school? people ask when they hear I went to school with the famous actor. *Do you remember?*

"He was geeky and funny and not part of any social group except the intellects and the people who were in acting class. He spelled him name Thom then. He had crazy curly hair and wore a dark olive army jacket from the Surplus store and was the best actor in all of the plays, especially South Pacific, where he played the sailor who has a ship tattooed on his stomach and rolls it around to impress the women on the island. He called me 'Sexy Sue' when he saw me in the halls, and he would pretend to smoke a cigar as he said it, tapping an imaginary ash. He was kind and funny and unpopular and two grades ahead of me. He laughed a lot. Great ass."

In the 1950s, steam ships stopped carrying people from San Juan Puerto Rico to New York City. My mother arrived on a steam ship when she was two. 1937.

Do you remember Puerto Rico? I ask her before I leave.

Phhhht. She says. *I remember nothing.*

Real Vintage Mink

I spilled kettle corn all over my microfiber blanket and spent an hour soaking it in dishwashing liquid and scooping off the kernels. This was kettle corn I bought for Christmas and opened just to have one bite, and it exploded all over my faux mink throw. All this before dawn. I text Augusten to ease the blow.

"Bwaby, go online and buy real vintage mink," Augusten says. "It's dirt cheap."

I tell him I feel anxious, as though I am constantly waiting for a hearse to roar up to my driveway with gaily colored balloons that say SO SORRY FOR YOUR LOSS and GET OVER IT.

"The only treatment is to write," he says. "That's the only way to be free of the feelings. It's horrible and unfair but true. Step out of the muck of the present and create your future."

The Liberator

Tom is liberating lady bugs from our bedroom. Carefully using his slightly spatulate forefingers as a ramp, an angle of escape for the lady bugs.

"Well, there's lots of different varieties of lady bugs," he says, though I have not asked. "There's quite a variety. There's like, two spot, three spot, six spot, four spot."

"So, they fly? Why don't they fly…" I say, watching them trudge up his finger plank. "Why are they always crawling around on all fours?"

"All sixes. Six legs. Because they're an insect. Just letting you know, that's all," he says.

I hand him a mini sandwich made from uncured salami and provolone cheese on a cracker smeared with mustard.

"Make me another one of those little sandwiches," he says immediately.

He is smiling and raising his blond eyebrows. They blend with his face. He has albino eyebrows. On someone else, they wouldn't work.

Once, Tom and I both heard a loud *THUNK* on the side of our house and then another *THUNK* like something hitting the ground. Tom stuck his head out the window of the living room to see a red-bellied sapsucker in the jaws of our neighbor's cat.

"BUDDY!" he said, just the one word, like a shot. Buddy dropped the woodpecker.

Tom hurried down into the back yard, picked it up, cradled it in his hands, and showed it to me as he was ferrying it to the front yard, where Buddy couldn't get it. The bird's head was sleek and a dark, Chinese red. He wasn't moving. Tom placed the bird on the lip of the garden, where the sunflowers grow.

My mother's life-size stone replica of Grumpy in *Snow White and the Seven Dwarfs* looked on with quiet disapproval. I go and stand next to the bird. "It doesn't look good," I say. He is not moving, laying like a pair of socks in the dirt. I sit cross-legged in front of the bird. I see now he is laying on his breast, his wings curled tightly around his body.

His beak is tan colored. I touch his glossy red head, as gently as possible. I settle in. It's warm, and the bees are buzzing around the sunflowers. Then I see his eye blink, or I think I see it. I wait for more, and I sit. One by one our dogs come. They look interested. I ask them to leave; they leave. Tom is behind me the whole time, holding a yellow mug of coffee, his fourth of the day.

"Can it fly?" he asks me, as though I'm in charge of this now.

I say, "I don't know. I think he is getting ready."

The bird seems to be gathering himself. He still has not moved from his breast in the dirt. But he is definitely alive—his eyes are open. I remain circumspect. I once watched a baby chipmunk die in this exact way. Tom steps forward and sort of lifts it all up, and the bird takes flight at once, not faltering. It crosses over the fence into the air, toward the skyline.

"Bye," I say.

"I could feel he was strong," Tom says. "I saved him."

"I know."

And it's not the first time. He once saved a Cooper's Hawk who collided with a car in front of our house. Stopped traffic, brought him into the house, wrapped him in a towel, and drove him to the place where hawks get mended, speaking quietly to him the whole time. I have seen him save snakes in the road, wayward turtles, lizards, and many a driveway frog by pausing and shining the lights and running around to scatter them before driving his truck into the garage. He would regularly release frogs from the deep drains at the swimming pool near where we lived. For ten years in his twenties, he had a pet turtle, a yellow-bellied slider named Hubert that grew too big and was set free to live in the wild at a golf pond. Two years later, he met up with Hubert while fishing. He knew him by a sickle shaped scar on his face. He told me that Humbert came right up to him, said *Thank you*, and lumbered off again. Free.

And the thing about Tom is he doesn't lie. He saw Hubert, and Hubert silently said *Thanks*. That's how it was.

Making A Pass

Dee and I are doing what she calls a Pass on my closet. Each item is taken out, displayed, and judged. One pile for clothes to donate, one pile for throwaways, and one pile for keeping. At the end of this process, another, more ruthless pass is performed.

"How many black dresses does one woman need?" Dee says, holding up a dark shroud.

"I love that dress. It's slimming."

"You can be buried in it. Just *no*," Dee says.

"Jesus," I say. Suddenly, I am Meryl Streep in World War II Poland, and someone is ripping a child away.

"You get to keep this one," she says next, holding up a slip dress in fuchsia. "You are a doll of life in this dress."

"And that one I got in New York…" I say, pointing to a green maxi.

"Get rid of it. Green isn't your color."

"Why?"

"Your skin has too much olive."

She's right.

"I have to keep that," I say, preempting Dee before she touches the next hanger.

"Why?"

"I got married in it," I say.

"No, you didn't. I was there," Dee says.

"I wore it to the reception," I say.

"So? Will you ever wear it again?"

"Maybe."

"It has puffed sleeves."

I say nothing. *It seemed like the thing to do at the time.* I mutter to myself. This is Uncle Pinkie's favorite expression, and one he used when he bought a Volkswagen van that was a lemon and drove it into a tree for the insurance, breaking a rib.

"Puffed sleeves," Dee repeats. "It's so Dorothy in *The Wizard of Oz.*"

I am not budging.

"All right," she says, making a new pile, the Clothes with a History pile. But she has a look in her eye that speaks to an eventual demise of the puffed sleeves. Dee will see to it.

We own about fifty things that are the exact same. Blouses. Pants. Dresses. Shoes. Accessories. Hats. We want to become like the famous twins in San Francisco, Marian and Vivian Brown, who dressed alike until they both died within a few months of one another. This is our goal.

Dee is a treasure I found.

My mother taught me about the power of friendship when I was a little girl.

"Any three women make a cone of power," she said.

"When?" I asked.

"Any time," she said. "Any place."

I remember she was folding laundry. Bunny ritualistically washed and dried and smoothed my clothes free of wrinkles, using only her hands. She buttoned every button.

As it happened, I had two close friends since kindergarten. We all three lived on the same street, on Jordan Road in Oakland. There was Dee, Colette, and me.

We became, I see now, a cone of power.

Over the years, one of us falls out with the other one with fair regularity.

But two women will do in a pinch.

In a pinch, one will do.

The Score

I have an Op-ed about my mother's loss of memory printed in the *New York Times*—on Mother's Day. It feels as though it was too easy. It feels like Bunny pushed it through.

I go to buy a hard copy at the newsstand. Then I tell Pablo to look online to read it. He texts me afterward:

DEMENTIA 0
NEW YORK 1

Once I started writing about Dementia and had a good therapist, a place to put the feelings, I stopped wishing my mother would die. I accepted everything exactly as it was, and most of my self-pity vanished.

And suddenly, here comes home hospice care and health aides. Here comes a lessening of suffering. Here comes the knowledge that this is her life, the one she was given…90 percent amazing, 10 percent completely unlooked for and fucked up, completely unknowable. In poker, I would keep this hand.

Ho Hos

I am at the supermarket, and I pick up a package of Hostess Ho Hos for my mom. Will she remember them? This is the constant game.

Oh, boy, she says the instant she lays eyes on them.

She doesn't remember who Ron is today, but she remembers Ho Hos. I feel really good about bringing them to her. As for the sugar and preservatives, well, fuck all that. The Bunny is out of the barn now; no use shutting the gate.

The Bank of Strength

There's this bank I go to, and it belongs to my mother. The Bank of Strength.

She's fading away, but there's still a lot in the bank, the bank that lives in her sacred core. When I am worried and heart sick, I go to the bank. I pick up the Fisher Price Chatter Phone and dial the number of their land line, which is now disconnected. (555) 733-9585. When she answers in that bright voice she always used, I say I need her to help me handle the refinancing of our house so we don't go broke. I need her advice on whether I am doing the right thing with my son, who has just totaled his car. I always think she's not there, but then here she comes. Handing me her strength.

The Marriage of Condiments

Tom likes to marry condiments and sauces and spreads. He will coerce the peanut butter jars into one big jar. If one is creamy and one chunky, it's of no consequence. It is the same with salsa. What matters is the union, the economy of space. Two things taking up necessary refrigerator space, both of like composition, let's say two bottles of salad dressing or chocolate syrup? They chafe. I'll come across him standing alone in his pajamas, officiating over the wedding of two chili sauce bottles, waiting with an air of patience and satisfaction. He takes pleasure in using the rubber scraper to get the last whorls of mayonnaise out of the older jar and transfer them to the new jar. You won't find him with unappreciated bits of stone ground mustard when there could be a marriage. He takes a close accounting of our refrigerator, and when we run out of something, he sounds the alarm.

"We're almost out of milk," he said last night. The worst news ever for Tom.

On the surface, this may not seem a plus. But there is something about the way he stands over two bottles of ketchup, making them kiss, becoming one. It soothes me. You never know what will do that. For this reason, you can never plan who to love or when. By the time you see him joining the tiny jars of capers, all advice is pointless.

Ryan O'Neal

In 2009, Ryan O'Neal hit on his daughter Tatum at Farrah Fawcett's funeral just moments after the hearse carrying his longtime love left the service.

"I had just put the casket in the hearse and was watching it drive away when a beautiful blond woman comes up and embraces me," O'Neal said. "I said to her, 'You have a drink on you? You have a car?' She said, 'Daddy, it's me, Tatum!'"

He said he was just trying to be funny with a strange Swedish woman. But it was his girlfriend's funeral. She was not even in the ground yet. He had just shoved the casket into the hearse, and before the taillights blinked, he was hunting pussy. It shouldn't be funny, but it is. He forgot his own daughter, and he didn't even have dementia. He had the leading actor's disease of only seeing yourself in the frame.

To even the karmic score, in 2020 he FaceTimed with a superfan with Alzheimer's named Robin. Every night before bed, she kissed the picture of Ryan on the DVD of *Love Story*.

To convince her it was truly him, he said, "Love means never having to say you're sorry."

Which is not true. In my experience, love means having to say you are sorry almost constantly.

When she realized it was indeed Ryan O'Neal, she said she was going to cry.

"Me too," Ryan said. And then he laughed.

Halloween

"That's it, let's go!" my mother says today.

"Go where?" Ron asks, sounding as though he is ready to pack.

"To die," she says.

Hi, ho, I think as I empty the trash. Here we go.

"What are you doing??" she barks at me.

"Helping Ron clean!"

"Who is she?" she asks Ron.

I was wondering who you were, I think.

I walk to her left side so she can see me. Her neck doesn't turn any more.

"It's me, Mom. I love you!"

I try to clean silently but knock over a recycling bin as I am putting out candy for the trick-or-treaters.

"WHAT ARE YOU DOING?"

"Losing my mind," I say gaily from the kitchen.

A long, high-pitched scream emanates from the living room. I have all the Halloween I can take, right here.

He Wants the Egg

My son calls. He tells me of the biodegradable egg, where you plant your loved ones under a tree in a Sacred Forest.

"Where?" I ask.

"The Sacred Forest. I think there are two or three."

"Really."

"Although it would be scary to visit a sacred forest because there are dead fetal people that are in utero just all under you. And they're not cremated; they're really there."

"I want cremation," I say.

"I want the egg. I want eternal life."

"You'll have that anyway. You're going to the right place," I say.

"Well, I still want the egg. I want my mass to convert into tree bark and stay in the earth."

"Why?"

"Because I feel like if the same molecules that are in my brain never leave the universe, if they specifically went into a tree? I feel like I would literally be in that tree. I would be like a tree person."

"You'd be an Ent, like in *Lord of the Rings*. That's good because we need more Ents," I say.

Our family watches the *Lord of the Rings* movies with regularity. We like the wizardry and the political gore.

"And instead of a million women or dads? The Ents could march on Washington and people would really listen."

Toon Blast

Today, I can't find a reason to leave the house. I get out my phone and play Toon Blast. There is a very expressive cartoon bear in the upper corner of the screen. He gets excited when I complete a level; he lifts a furry fist in the air. He looks sad when I lose and run out of lives. He hangs his head.

I run out of lives. I pivot to Toy Blast. Here there are pink pigs that pop up and need to be destroyed in order to level up, a certain amount of them in a limited number of moves. I am playing Level 5,742, and I think I'm winning, but then I realize that there are more targets than are immediately visible. I feel betrayed.

"The pigs just keep on coming," I say to Dee later. I know she will understand.

"Fucking pigs," she says.

Gone with the Wind

My mother will begin speaking to her dead father, sometimes with playfulness. Sometimes in fear.

"When are we going home, Daddy?"

This is where she lives now. Her childhood in New York City, where she was cherished and photographed by her father Ferdinand, dead since 1951.

Today, I play evocative music from the seventies, her most favorites. Tom Jones's *Live at Las Vegas*. Aretha Franklin's *Lady*

Soul. I try to lure her forward in time to where we are. I play an audio recording of *Gone with the Wind* for her. She is patient for a couple of minutes and then says *No.* Gently suggesting that she is done with all that nonsense.

A faint cloud of insipient death hovers over me after I leave my parent's house. I can feel it, the way dirt surrounded Pigpen. I have breakthrough techniques. I run. I cook, bringing plates of rosemary lemon chicken and bowls of refried beans to my parents. I write.

I look deeply into the face of my little dog, Colette. Her nicknames are Fluffernutter, Little Fat Dog, and Cowlettentott. She is a papillon breed with huge, soft butterfly ears and a little bullet body. A tail that waves like the world's furriest flag, an intelligent face like a lemur. What I see looking back at me cheers me on a cellular level. As I go about my day, I would like to wear her like a fluffy stole. But she follows me from room to room, saying *WE GOOD, WE GOOD,* in the international language of dogs. I think about the Ojibwe saying: "Sometimes I go about in pity for myself, and all the while, a great wind carries me across the sky."

The Dancer

I'm driving down College Avenue, and I see a well-groomed elderly man off to my left, crossing Ashby. He crosses in graceful strides, his arms outstretched and curved, as though embracing the day. He's doing an occasional twirl, pretty good ones. He dances through the intersection, wearing khakis and an orange raincoat and a sky-blue baseball cap.

I know his brain is flawed, but my first impulse is to follow him. To know what he knows.

The Judge

I get a jury summons. I resolve to serve, but when I get there, I discover that it's a murder case, possibly several months long. My parents trump this. I have to evade of jury selection.

"A self-employed writer! What do you write?" the Judge asks.

"Made-up stories," I say.

"What genre of books do you write?"

"I've never thought about it."

"Mystery? Romance?"

"Women's Fiction," I say, as though I am saying *skin tag* and pulling aside a hospital gown.

"And you spent twenty years in the advertising industry," the Judge says. "What did you do?"

"I made up stories."

I am sticking to a very few words so as not to be tricked.

"What kind of stories?"

"Persuading people to buy things they don't need," I say.

He barrels on, his thin white head a lie detector needle.

"And in the advertising, you use psychology to make the ads, using images and colors to persuade people to buy things. Can you listen to a witness and not persuade them to your way of thinking?"

"I don't understand," I said. "You just equated writing ads with being a psychologist."

"Can you listen to the case evidence presented without bias?"

"Well," I say. "I can't appreciate a judicial and police system built on the back of slavery. So no, I can't be neutral."

The judge is mad, but I don't look at him. They will you to comply with their eyes and their ebony robes of doom.

"If a family member were to be brought to trial, would you want their jurors to be neutral?"

I pretend to think about this.

"No..." I say, as though I am declining a second martini.

None of the lawyers have any questions for me. I think I am released, but the judge announces that we all have to come back in ten days for Jury Selection. The song "Poor Unfortunate Souls" from *The Little Mermaid* rings through my mind. Ursula wants us all back there in ten days.

When I go back in ten days, the lawyers don't look at me. I am dismissed. I should feel ashamed, but it is year four in Dementia. I have only a few feelings left.

Smoke

I used to smoke. It helped me cope.

Years ago, a friend's son was in a bad skateboard accident. Willi, fourteen. And she right away started smoking, non-filters, sometimes two at once. Leaving the ICU to have one after another after another. She liked the feel of the tobacco against her teeth as she prayed, she told me.

The first day, they took off the left side of his skull to ease the pressure. And my friend said it was good, and that she never would have guessed half a skull would be beneficial. She said smoking was a furtive act, and all the nurses did it. She spent hours on the roof of the parking garage with the nurses, chain smoking while her son was in ICU. It reminded me of nuns gathering with the dying before the priest is called in to say the last rites. A cigarette communion. The sacrament of the Bic lighter.

This morning, I seriously considered both smoking and the single old Xanax I found in the bottom of my purse. But then what? They can't save me. Yes, I could take it, but then I would just wake up back in my own life. I will save it for the funeral.

I feel fondness for the woman who used to smoke. She too has passed.

As for Willi, he lived.

It may be that his brain stopped bleeding at just the right moment, a supreme piece of luck. It may be that as his mother and the nurses smoked, they pulled him back by the tips of his toes and sent his death whirling into the air.

No One Dies in Lily Dale

I find seven metal Buddhas and assorted holy men in a large Tupperware in her office, the room where she gave readings. I bring it home and set them all up on my nightstand, like sentinels. The madness of her house has now fully leaked over to my house. I am in the processing of fully becoming her.

Meanwhile, Ron is getting me a high-resolution copy of *No One Dies in Lily Dale*, so that I can guess the imposters from the psychics.

"Wait until you see the medium from Florida with the stripper high heels," he says.

"Did Mom watch?"

"For about ten minutes, then she closed shop."

When Bunny closes shop, she simply draws a blanket over her face and goes inward, sleeping her way to betterment.

Late that night, I watched *No One Dies in Lily Dale*, starring an astonishing array of quacks with the occasional true medium thrown in. I feel Dementia and Lily Dale could connect by an adjoining isthmus. Will I too set sail to Dementia? Is my name on the manifest? I don't know, but I have started to set aside any discarded pills I find in the pharmacy of their bathroom. Because it seems as though Bunny has been caught unawares and is standing in deep water. I watch myself doing this. I plan not to kill myself but to simply stay incredibly stoned if it happens.

After midnight, Tom bumped into the nightstand, upsetting most of the Eastern religious figurines. The sound was like the crack of tiny guns.

Claudia Speaks

"I know I shouldn't, but I feel pretty good," I say. "Yesterday? I gave away twenty bags of clothes and shoes and belongings. I may be done grieving."

"Mmmmm," she says.

Where is my affirmation?

"This is really big," she says, shaking her head back and forth. Claudia seems to be looking at something very sad, like a dead kitten.

"I have a surge of energy, and I just feel very much lighter. I just didn't realize how ready I was to let all of this go. Wow."

There is a beat as she adjusts her glasses.

"You have to go through all the stages, Suzanne."

Claudia launches this truth missile and waits for me to unveil more of myself. She sits and waits. I give her nothing.

"Of course," I say with a wide rictus grin.

Inside, I am in denial. I feel I can skip the stages, or at least fast-forward. The stages, I reason, don't apply to Dementia. I will be able to phone in the stages.

But no, now I can see that this is why I'm here, and she is right. *You Have to Go Through All the Stages* is now an ugly Quaker sampler in my head. As I drive, it's a car flag riffling in the air.

Now I keep walking in and out of rooms, looking for something. I don't want to grieve, not all at once and certainly not now when there is so much to do. And yet Claudia said I have to go through the stages. How best to do this without feeling anything?

I may need even more pills, stronger pills. Lobotomy pills. And I may need to get back in touch with Nadine Blackman, the DeGriefer.

DeGriefing

I am Zooming with my grief therapist of old, Nadine, who saved me in 2000. Recently, I realized I needed a second therapist in addition to Claudia. I don't just need the ACE bandage; I need the tourniquet. I don't just need one kind of pie; I need all the pie.

I found Nadine again on Google. Her grey, wiry hair curls around her face as her large black eyes beam at me.

"So, what's happening today? You went to your parents' this morning, and your stepdad was there?"

"Yes. I had a good visit yesterday. I cut my mom's hair. I washed it with dry shampoo. I cut her hair, and she let me."

I am five years old; my mother is trimming my bangs. She is wearing an orange sweatshirt; my father has a matching sweatshirt. My bangs are crooked for all of my school pictures. I am happy.

"How long was she married to your father?"

"Fourteen years, and then my dad left her when I was seven."

"Is it a vivid memory for you?"

"Not really," I say.

A red plaid suitcase. The sound of a door closing. A dark foyer. Me waiting for the door to open again and for my father to reappear in a magical way. Which he did from time to time. To sleep with my mother and then leave again, like the Sandman, high on Scotch sodas.

"When you wake up and she's the first thing on your mind, what happens to you?"

"I feel numb. I feel like I've been sort of acting my way through the last few years. But I have my best friend who I can share everything with, and I have my husband."

"I want to know about him. The new one."

The old husband was what sent me to Nadine in 2000. He's the one that Nadine helped me degrief from. After he, too, left his wife and child: a family tradition I faithfully followed. Nadine scraped me off the killing floor and threw me back in the air, and eventually, I took wing to Tom.

"He's great. He helps with my parents. Never complains. But there's a filter when I talk to him. He rarely discusses emotions. I have to pry them out of him with a stick."

"It's interesting with the names here are playing with. My present husband is Ron," she says.

Her present husband is Ron, and she is seventy-three. How many is she planning on having? How I admire Nadine.

"I married him last January. I had a kidney stone. My very dear friend Richard was visiting from Brooklyn and so was Ron, both of whom I have known for thirty years. So, Richard is having breakfast with us, and he looks at Ron and he says, 'You should marry her.' And I expect Ron at seventy-eight to say, 'I didn't marry my whole life. I don't need to marry.' And he said, 'How do we do it?'"

"He was ready," I say.

Like Tom, I think, who proposed after five weeks. Despite the fact that he was still married, although his wife had decidedly set sail. He didn't let the fact that he was married stop him from getting engaged. Which is also very Brooklyn.

"Suzanne, the truth of marrying at my age means, *I'm here for your death.*"

Nadine throws both hands into the air, fingers splayed. As though she is catching Death with both hands.

"How long has Ron been your dad?"

"Since my dad left. My mom was beautiful, vivacious. And she fell in love with Ron. He worked in the mail room of the company where she was a secretary. And so, it's been fifty-five years."

Bunny was at work and had forgotten her hair comb. She asked Ron for one. He loaned his comb to her. No doubt this was some sort of low-key brujeria. The next day, he gave her a bag of plastic combs shaped like fish in many colors. Ron began to be a gentle presence, bringing Chinese food to our apartment in Oakland. Gave us all the fish combs in the universe. Never left. He was twenty-six. She was thirty-four.

"Okay. That is speaking to me," Nadine says. "He's shielding you from the real worry about your mother because of his care and the hospice. But you certainly carry the empathic sense of your mother's moment-to-moment departure."

"When my first husband Mark was dying, it was very easy for me to embrace his parents. It was his third battle with cancer. Ironically, he married me when the CAT scan showed no cancer. And of course, it was in there hiding."

Another thief, I think. Watching and waiting. Like dementia. Like Prometheus, stealing fire and passing it around eagerly to burn down the world.

"I want to differentiate between somatic resonance and genetic resonance. Somatic resonance is you feeling your best friend's pain and becoming her pain—versus the genetic resonance that comes with blood relationships, and is much worse in terms of pain."

"Oh, boy," I say.

Nadine ploughs right along.

"So, when I would embrace his mom or his dad, there would be a sense of service and love. It was a somatic resonance. But when my sister Donna was dying of cancer, hugging my mother was one of the more painful experiences I've had in my life because we're connected by genetics, by DNA. So, the genetic resonance was intense and darkly profound. As you have with your mother. It's an absolute cellular ache in the middle of one's being when it's flesh and blood. It's the woman who bore you. It can't get more primal."

"You wake up, Tom's there, and you know you're loved. He knows he's loved. And then there's the rest of the story. And since you can't fix, rescue, or save your mom, the shift must be within you. A conscious decision. Because we don't get over our losses. A mom dying this way is a loss."

Wait, we don't get over our losses? This feels like news. Bad news but also, in a way, good news. I needn't try to get over this. I can just let it wash over me, like battery acid. Like a hard, necessary rain.

"I want to know just a little bit about your beloved present, delicious husband. Just give me one sentence about him." Nadine says.

I think about this.

Every night for the year we were engaged, I grew anxious. I'd ask Tom, *What's going to happen to us?* And he would say, *We are going to be happy for the rest of our lives.*

Memory

In *Thinking About Memoir*, Abigail Thomas writes that the word *memory* comes from the same root as the word *mourn*, and that should tell us something.

She says that there's always a side door that leads into what you want to write about. That in her late age, she started writing about things she had never written about before.

The future is a moving target, she writes, *as is the past.*

I am trying to hang onto this final time with my mother and name it, but it is elusive. Because in fact, she is sliding past me and away from me and also rushing to me and toward me. Like a great river I am standing in with a bucket, I will only catch some of it.

THREE

What Remains

We shall find peace. We shall hear angels.
We shall see the sky sparkling with diamonds.

Anton Chekhov

The Approach

I am carrying *coquito* to Hayward, a Christmas gift I ferry earlier each year. I brewed the spices today. Cloves, cinnamon. Star anise. Ron generally doesn't drink, but coquito brings him joy.

There is no way to know what I will find when I come to see her, she who was once as constant as the sun. I could call any time, and her voice would be bright, amused. The sun.

I will enter the house of mystery again. The knowledge handed me fresh each time, at the door: you will lose things, and not the way you wanted. Parents first. Then lovers. Possibly, children. The Devil has legs. But this is where family is. This is love. Come in. Take the hit.

On the approach to my parent's house, I begin the ritual. I stop the car at the entrance to the gates of their senior mobile home community, Spanish Ranch II. I take a breath and push fear from my mind, though it is there. I drive forward. Park my car. Open the door. Cry a joyous hello, no matter what I find. Become my mother.

The After

My son FaceTimes. I tell him about what is happening in Dementia.

He says he believes that Grandma is going to a good place after this.

But sometimes I don't believe there will be an after. I can't see it.

"You don't see Morocco either," he says. "But millions of people have been to Morocco."

We laugh. Water in the desert.

Walter Mercado

Bunny talks to ghosts on the ceiling. Ron wakes up and sometimes tapes it on his phone. We are searching for clues. We trust her process.

Always, she has been unafraid of ghosts. Other people pay money to rid their houses of spirits, always avoiding a house where someone has died. Not Bunny. She welcomed the intrusion.

She never missed Walter Mercado's horoscopes on Telemundo. When he did his predictions, no one was allowed to speak. Together, we watched him grow old and stay young with a sequined cape, watched him sail into paroxysms of joy and fearful warnings and then reverse course like a hurricane, sparing some and not others. He was Boricua Liberace, an eyeliner prophet. Walter Mercado knew things about you, be you Virgo or Taurus or Scorpio; he knew things every day.

Walter Mercado was bruja. How we need his wise counsel now.

I Can't Do Anything

I'm washing dishes, and I hear my mother cry out in anguish. *I can't do anything!*

I hear her frustration and fury, but after several years, I have stopped matching it in emotion. I hear it, and I send out a thin candy shell of protection around myself so as to go on being there.

I don't tell you about a lot of this. I can't see how it would help raise the tide.

I bring her a sippy cup with mango smoothie. I tell her mangos are from Puerto Rico, and that's why we love these. She smiles a wan smile and says, *Thank you, Tutti.* All is well again. I lower my shields.

Nadine and the Assumptive World

Today, I tell Nadine my mother was recently approved for hospice and home healthcare, which took a lot of the load of worry off my stepdad and me.

Nadine lifts one finger up in the air.

"Okay. We're going to replace that word, *worry.* We're going to use the word *focus, attend to, serve, check up on, keep, stay vigilant with*—because worry in and of itself gives the mind a different intention. Worry can be described as ruminating and using precious energy about something that may or may not ever happen."

Nadine dives right into our sessions. She is like a very thin sumo wrestler who doesn't need to warm up.

"Let's transform the use of that worrying concept. Let's take the anxiety out of the word we use because *worry* produces anxiety. Just the word itself really upsets the system."

I tell her my mother shows zero signs of dying. That she is still oddly strong, like a worn cloth doll with wire inside. That Bunny could easily go two more years.

"Yes. But it's dangerous if you assume that you know what's going to happen next. It's an assumption. But the assumptive world is part of how the psyche maintains some sums of hope. We assume our parents won't suddenly lose their minds and become bedridden. And so, the assumptive world was shattered for you. This is why when you wake up, you think, *Oh no.* But since you can't fix rescue or save Bunny, you really just serve her. And on some level, that's how we describe palliative care. Palliative care is the shift. It's the shift from saving the body to serving the being."

I think about my mother's body, grown so much smaller in her age. The way she shuns clothing of any kind now and is simply swathed in just a robe and blankets. The smooth yet stretched skin that falls around her in soft waves the color of wheat.

"People are telling me, 'Try not to worry.' But how?" I say.

Nadine raises another finger into the air. It's a multi-finger-session. The best kind.

"Trying is an excuse for doing. So, I don't encourage people to choose the word *try*. Instead, I ask them to consider it and let me know. *Consider* it. Don't try it. Consider it."

Consider not worrying. Consider not caring. Consider not existing. This could go, it seems to me, in a variety of different directions.

"We talked about you waking up and having this feeling of dread. So, we need to create what's called the *sankalpa*: an intention formed by the heart and mind. It's a projection into the future of what one wants rather than what's happening. For example, I've had two rotator cuff surgeries. And when I would get scared about my shoulder not healing, I'd come to, *I heal well.* So that's my main sankalpa. And it would remind me that anything else other than staying with that was a waste of my momentary energy and time."

Nadine stretches her arms overhead and clasps her hands for the counter stretch, extending her neck forward like a dancer. She is a match for any surgery one could name. She must stay limber and well to save people. And so, God writes her a hall pass. I inwardly thank Him.

"So when that first breath is there, and you open your eyes, sankalpa is a statement of what's happening in the present with the intention to serve oneself with how we tell it."

"My mother is on her path," I say. It doesn't even take me a second to come up with my sankalpa. As though it was waiting like an umbrella at my fingertips.

"Excellent. You are being challenged to communicate with the umbilical force that has you so bonded to her. And it also gives you an opportunity to be the observer, the responsive person rather than the reactive person. Nostril breathing is another key, I promise you. Nostril breath keeps panic and anxiety at a minimum. It airs the third eye and the pineal gland, which is one of the master regulators of the endocrine system. So just by nostril breathing, there is an intention to clarify before reacting."

I try to breathe through my nostrils, but they are clogged. I resolve to buy Afrin.

"You're being asked to take a breath and acknowledge your mother is on her path. You're putting it in a more neutral zone of the unknown."

Nadine raises another finger in the air. Sensing a shift in the wind.

"Let's prove it. If I challenge you now, is there something that you should be doing? Is there is one thing that you should be doing right now that Bunny needs that you're not attending to?"

"No," I say. Because there isn't.

Relief hits me like a corsage thrown by a bride. I catch it.

A Spell of Longing

"I'm getting out of here," Bunny says, triumphant.

"When can we go home?"

"Where am I?"

We assure her that she is home. This is it.

"I didn't think she would last this long," Ron says. "The doctors predicted a year at most."

We are keeping her alive, a kind of spell. A spell of longing.

I start riding my old bike, which takes me back in time. I'd forgotten how much riding a bike is like flying.

As I pedal, I think, *I am well, I am well.* A prayer of monstrous hope and gratitude.

Magic Is All Around

Today, I felt vibrantly alive and thankful to see my mom still. To be able to. We tell each other we love each other again and again. She asks about my husband. It's one of her safe sentences that she still knows. Whenever Tom pops up in the Parade of Faces, she perks up and says, "Who's that?" My mother likes men. She always has. When her grown grandson appears in the Parade, he is a stranger. She only knows him as a child. Dementia erased her grandson as cleanly as a light pencil mark on paper.

Yet when we walked in together on his last visit, she remembered. Pablo played many songs on his guitar and sang softly to her; she was soothed and did not grow impatient. We'd flown him out from Asheville for a week after a year apart. Fuck the pandemic. We're living, here.

When I am at her house, back with my family of origin, I am outside of myself. I never think of problems; I only Do.

Ron and I planted more succulents in the planters on the back deck. They appeared to Tom and me last night on our walk: six healthy plants, their edges vermillion and their faces bright green, with a scrap paper sign marked FREE SUCCULENTS AND STUFF. A small purple beehive vase, no chips.

Magic is all around now that the end appears to be nigh. I greedily take it all. The succulents and the stuff.

Clean

In my mother's vernacular, nothing was ever just dirty; it was filthy. If I complimented her on the cleanliness of her home, she would demur, saying, "My mother's house: now, *that* was clean."

When I moved into a new apartment or house, she came to do the kitchen. She brought a cleaning caddy filled with rags and Pine-Sol and Spic and Span. She bustled about unwrapping dishes and washing them, carefully lining shelves. Her own she trimmed with white plastic lace.

She used to rearrange furniture in the middle of the night. We would wake up to a new living room, somehow vastly improved yet with the same pieces. In the '70s, she found an antique potbellied stove and placed it in the corner, bright plastic daisies in its belly. She created order wherever she went and recognized disorder in the seemingly perfect. I once showed her a picture of a deeply handsome man I was unsure of.

"There's something wrong with his face," my mother said, and turned away to sweep her floors.

She can't walk to another room and see if it's right now. She lives in one room and will until she dies. But I know what she would want. I don a headscarf and pink rubber gloves. I start from the corners of the kitchen floor and work my way to the center on my hands and knees. This is the only way. I was a maid once, as was every woman in my Puerto Rican family. I come from a long line of high priestesses disguised as cleaning women from an archipelago in the Caribbean. I know what I'm doing and why.

Remember

For those who travel often to Dementia, dread is all around, like oxygen. And how do you breathe something else? Because you must, or else you will collapse in your tracks.

You walk in nature. You stay away from the future. You love and are silent when it comes to complaints, which do no good and soil the air. You remember, which is to say, put your mother back together again through memories. The time we ran in the rain in Boston with empty pizza boxes on our heads. The moment she silently and artfully tipped the loose crystal off the chandelier at The Parker House with the tip of her umbrella, with a look of studied innocence, so that she could collect it "as a souvenir."

You get a Claudia or a Nadine…or both, if you can. Somewhere to put the feelings. And when the terrain gets darker, you get a second therapist, a specialist, one just for grief.

I have that stolen crystal hanging on thread in my little writing room. In the morning, it splays rainbows across the wall. The graffiti of love, remembered.

Fuck Off

I wait until Ron is out of the room, and then I tell my mother about this memoir. I tell her how much I want it to be published because it is the story of our family. I am trying to get her to encourage me and believe in me the way she used to. I need it.

She looks at me blankly. *The well is empty*, she seems to be saying. *Fuck off.*

But I don't give up. Why would I give up?

I tell her I am not afraid.

"I'm not afraid, Mommy," I say.

But I lie.

A few weeks later, I try again.

"But could it happen, Mommy? Could the memoir be published?"

Her eyes have glazed over.

"Why not?" she says.

It is no longer appropriate that I ask for anything from my mother.

I used to be able to answer the phone at my mother's house and be her. I would listen and respond for about a minute and then say, *Hold on,* and hand the phone to my mother.

I look more like her every day. If I catch my reflection unaware, I can be slapped by the fact of her face on mine, a transparency.

Heads turned when she entered a room. This used to happen to me. We were taught to be visible and appealing to the eye, and then, at a certain age, we became invisible. Now we are old together; now we are invisible together.

We are the lucky ones.

The Four Moons of Jupiter

Tom says to come see Jupiter in the front yard. He has brought the telescope and set it up so that I can see it.

Initially, I can't see it, but then I can. It's orange, and there are four brightly colored specks around it: its moons.

When he Googles it, he finds that there are, in fact, eighty moons around Jupiter.

We also see Saturn and the rings around Saturn, a shimmering white bar.

I didn't want to come out into the yard because it was cold and because I was on my phone. I would have missed it. Who knows when the planets are this close again?

It strikes me that living in Dementia is like barely seeing the four moons of Jupiter when really there are eighty. But does it matter if you see all eighty?

Mrs. Piggle-Wiggle's Magic

I lost a book from the Oakland Library at Fruitvale when I was small. I'd checked it out many times; it was a close friend. I looked everywhere, and it seemed to eight-year-old me that losing a library book was one of the worst crimes one could commit. I dragged my cheap dresser away from the wall to look, but nothing. I was obsessed with finding it, as though it were a genie lamp.

Last night, I dreamt I found that book. I saw the book jacket: Mrs. Piggle-Wiggle with her stout back to the viewer, neighborhood children gathered around her. The tip of her magic wand sparkled in the air. It made me feel safe and happy. I admired Mrs. Piggle-Wiggle so much and loved her like a real person. The way she married a pirate, Mr. Piggle-Wiggle, who died after a long and happy life and left her a chest full of cash. The way she smoothly, without them even knowing it, made everyone in her life better via witchcraft. Especially the children. Children were malleable. They would eat what was given them, so long as it tasted of caramel syrup or bubble gum. The Bully Cure. The Interrupter Cure. Mrs. Piggle-Wiggle performed them all on the children of her town. Some magical remedies came in powders and some came in potions, and some were strictly behavioral. Some of the names of the children in the book were Paraphernalia Grotto and Nicholas Semicolon. Sylvia Quadrangle.

This was a witch who had all the trappings of a normal household, a household with a farm and lots of chocolate cake and so forth. This was the household I thought I wanted when I was a young girl, in order to fit in.

I see now that the house we had was the only right house. And in fact, Mrs. Piggle-Wiggle was just my Abuelita in drag.

The Lavender Gnome

Dee has come for the weekend, and we are driving and listening to *Stillness Speaks*, a top track in our spiritual hit parade by Eckhart Tolle. We call him ET or The Lavender Gnome because he's small, and his book jackets and Instagram feature a lot of lavender.

The Lavender Gnome says that the secret of life is to die before you die and find that there is no death, in which case Bunny is way ahead of the curve.

"Silence is the language God speaks. Everything else is a bad translation…" he says.

(beat)

One man in the audience laughs maniacally.

"At this moment? Silence is teaching," says the Lavender Gnome.

Today is Saturday. Later, the Jehovah's Witnesses knock on the door. Dee and I continue listening. Eventually, they go away, the Witnesses, shuffling in their black suits and church clothes. They always travel in groups.

The Lavender Gnome says the most important statement in the Bible is "Be still and know I am God." He says that when you are here now, and your mind is in the future, it creates an anxiety gap. The trick is to stay out of the gap and to be present.

Dee slaps the sofa with her hand. "This is where it's at."

"But is this all there is?" I say. Disappointed. Hopeful.

"Yes," she says.

Ecstasy

Church again. It heals me.

As I drive home from Saint Andrew today across the bay, I gaze at the sun on the water, and I realize I am in religious ecstasy. It makes no sense because this is not in a happy time in my life. But still the ecstasy came, and I felt drenched in the holy spirit. I called Dee and told her, she who I have occasionally prayed with on my knees; something we would be too embarrassed to do with anyone else. But Dee and I are the same person, so there is no shame.

I think about how Ram Dass says we are not the ripples on the ocean; we are the ocean. We are not the winds that disrupt the surface; we are the still depth that never changes.

Benediction

The succulents I planted in Ron's planter boxes on their back deck are overgrown; their thick, long, green arms reach out to the back door as if to breach it. I prune and sweep, and now the back deck is airy and pleasant again. Ron likes to sit here and smoke cigars, sometimes a little weed, though he is seventy-seven—even though my mother never did, nor did she drink past her mid-thirties. There is no reason for all this, a fact I recycle again and again.

Ron has planted mint. I give it its own place with the basil and rosemary. He has kept the house up well, and so I don't do maid service this trip; I do outdoor work.

"Who's that!?" my mother says when she sees me on my way out.

"Bye, Mommy. I love you," I say quickly.

"I love you too," she says after a moment.

I can't remember her laugh anymore.

I have reached a high point of sadness, where hope is lost and love turns in on itself, a city in Dementia that all reach no matter who they are or what they bring to protect themselves.

What will I need, I suddenly wonder, to pack myself out of this country when this is over? I haven't considered this because part of me believes it will never end, like a spell in Brothers Grimm.

"It will end," my son says. A benediction.

I need to begin to let go of my mother and my grown son on an opposite coast. I imagine standing on a hill with two balloons, letting them go.

My brother let go of my mother's balloon and my balloon long ago. I want to go to his house and ask, "How did you do it? What is your secret?"

I imagine him not answering the door. I imagine him opening the door. So, two more balloons. One for the brother I knew as a child and one for the stranger he became.

Nadine and the Fifth Chamber

I am Zooming with Nadine. It's 5:00 p.m., and I am in my pajamas. This way, I don't have to change clothes all day and night and into the next day. This way, the hamper stays empty.

She hooks into this right away, providing triage.

"So I want to, on a golden platter, give you the word *wonder* to regularly use every morning and throughout the day. Just, *I'm wondering,* as in *I wonder what Bunny's end of life will look like? I wonder how I will do Christmas this year?* While you're wondering, you're loving, and you're caring. You're not doting, fretting, and hovering.

"There's just no quick fix. How do you make meaning of these moments while you're both still alive but she is compromised? Watch out for your tricky mind playing games with you, insisting that this should be easy. You have a heavy lesson going on, and you're overwhelmed.

"I'm going to give it another name, and that is *Compathy*. Compathy is an overload of compassion and empathy. But you can't change what's happening. Only your relationship to it. Remember, we don't get over our losses. I never want to get over my sister Donna. She lives in the fifth chamber of my heart. There's two arteries and two ventricles. The fifth chamber is the metaphoric chamber where our loved ones live."

It's their own little motor lodge where they drive their soul Ferraris in and park. It's an inner Four Seasons where we can visit them and know that they are deep into spa treatments. It's the Free Parking space in the Monopoly board, the tree in the yard that children playing Hide and Seek run to and touch, shouting *Home!* with their faces alight.

"When your mom passes, your work could be to invite her right into this fifth chamber. And anytime you take your left hand and cover it with your right hand and place them over your heart, you send compassion to self, and she's right there."

"It's good we're talking about death," I say. "Because what I notice when things are at their worst with my mom, I feel like I am dying. And whenever the phone rings, it's a cattle prod. It feels like everything is a lethal situation. And right now, my dramatic thought is *I can't live through this again.* Not with my husband, not with my friends, not with myself, not with anyone."

"Right," Nadine says, nonplussed. "That's purely the mind. It's the hysterical mind shouting that we can't live through this again. *Really?* We've done it before. And if we need to, we'll do it again."

Nadine is tough. Nadine is an OG.

"When we are fragile from so much, grief scatters and shatters linear thinking. Everything is altered."

I make her repeat it.

"Grief scatters and shatters linear thinking."

I think of this as a temporary tattoo. I think of it as a car flag, riffling through the air while I drive to the drug store without my wallet.

"But why is it that when anything goes wrong, my kneejerk thought now is just Death?"

"Because it exists, and it is being driven home because your mother is dying. This is bereavement overload. But also? You are expanding."

The words of an E. E. Cummings poem chime in my mind: when he describes how the ears of his ears are awake, and the eyes of his eyes are open.

Secret Fort

When Tom was ten, he and two friends, Johnny Kazinsky and his brother Ira, dug a little room, the secret fort. It was like a wide grave. Deep enough for several young boys to sit in. They covered it with a piece of plywood that could be lifted. Every day before they left, they covered it with freshly trampled down leaves and weeds and sticks. They had to camouflage it so no one could commandeer it or steal things. They would sit in it and smoke cigarettes and read *Playboy* magazines and talk about girls. That's where they did their best caper plotting, which often entailed their friend Donnie Taylor stealing twenty dollars so they could go to Carvel's, whose mascot was an octopus, and buy hot fudge sundaes. Or go buy an Estes Rocket to set off in the woods. According to Tom, the rockets would go up about a thousand feet, either shooting straight up or shooting sideways and spearing a child's head. "It was mostly up," he said.

Then the rockets would smash back down into the ground, and he'd rebuild them.

I laughed as he described the part about the sticks and trampling the leaves over the plywood, and he looked at me and said, very seriously, "You've obviously never built a secret fort."

And I never had. But I have one now. These pages.

Turning

Today, she said, apropos of nothing, "I'd love to go to Puerto Rico."

My mother, who never says she wants to go anywhere and must be roused to speech. Who never, even when she was well and lithe, showed interest in going back to the place where she was born, and for good reason. The heat. The abandonments. The *barrio*.

Now she wants to go back. People are suffering all over the island tonight, but she wants to go. She would love to go.

Is she turning toward home? Now her ship is small, agile. She can decide, no matter how late.

I find a small, heart-shaped tin of human hair in her desk drawer. It's not mine. It's fine, light brown. And it is soft. Like baby hair. In my mind, I see her taking it from my son with a small scissors two decades ago. My mother tenderly snips some hair, thinking, *I may need this later.*

My mother was a fortuneteller, but she didn't see this trip to Dementia coming.

However.

She did say she would die at eighty-one, a very specific number, and the year in which she was finally diagnosed.

Into the West

Ritualistically, I listen to the London Philharmonic play music from *The Hobbit*. I stream the whole *Lord of the Rings* soundtrack as loud as I like, and I throw things away. Every day, I discard. I donate. I reorganize not just my parents' house but my own. I reorganize my life without my mother or children.

"Hope fades…" is particularly apt. But then the music builds to a crescendo, and Annie Lennox goes into high priestess mode and starts to roar.

The whole soundtrack—and especially this song—are beautiful to me. Because that's where I am now, a kind of battle. I must transition and have a completely blind faith in some hidden outcome, some magic ring, or the lack of it. I have to clatter about and bumble my way through this darkness to get there, past demons and the inner critic, who is relentless.

This portion of the war is hard. I am halfway in and halfway out, and I can't go back. And there is so little energy left to move forward. But I must, or simply give up and die. As if death were that simple and innocuous. If so, I surely would have pulled a lever long ago, the one marked BAIL. Pulled the fuck out of it.

Instead, I sing along, face wet with tears. I go through the involuntary rebirth canal, sailing over the River Styx with a fat, splintery oar. I am just gutting it out. Increasingly, I see there is freedom in surrender. There's music.

Fly Fishing

Years ago, Tom tried to teach me fly-fishing. I broke the rod. I fell on it with my entire body weight. He got another one. I broke that one.

I blamed the rods—as strong as a breadstick! Sturdy as a blade of grass!

I disliked the equipment hanging all over me, the boots and the waders and the vest full of bullshit. I needed the river to stop running so fast so I could learn. *I can't stand this* is what I was thinking as it repeatedly pushed me down. Under my feet, river stones slick with algae tried to topple me from the other direction.

I laid down in a shady patch on the riverbed, emptying my waders. Tiger swallowtails float above me, eating the blackberries that are ripening, going from a hard red to a fat, moist ebony. Dragonflies look like airplanes from where I lay on the cool soil; bees come and bumble all around me. I feel at home on my back on the edge of the riverbed. In the river, Tom is standing firm, casting and whipping his rod around like a magician's wand. He cries out with joy when he gets one on his line. He will catch the iridescent fish with a red racing stripe down its side. He will measure it against his rod before throwing it back after a brief conversation where the fish is praised and admired.

He has never broken a rod. He has never kept a fish.

He wanders upstream. I take everything off. The waders, the double socks. The boots with their Velcro bottoms. I carry it all back to the truck.

I sit in the parking lot in Oroville while meth deals blossom around me. It is over a hundred degrees. I turn the air conditioning on; I turn it off. The same rumbling cars with tinted windows come and go, looking nonchalant while the very thin people rush toward them. It will be many hours before Tom is through. I am thinking how selfish and self-centered he is, how I actually may be robbed and killed like a bystander in *The Wire*.

When I see him walking back, his old leather hat on his head, I feel a helpless joy.

It is what I feel now, realizing I get to walk my mother home.

Rise

Today, my mother didn't know who I was and shouted until I left the house. As I drive home, I am crying so hard I can't breathe and must pull over. But also, there is relief. To have hit some bottom.

Three days later, I go back.

I give myself permission to not visit with my mother and only administer to Ron if I get too afraid.

I walk in and say, "Hi, Mommy!"

Her eyes are clear.

"Hi, Tutti," she says.

"I love you!" I say.

"Oh, I love you too."

I know this is only one of the first rooms that lead into Hell, that lead into me having to let her go. But I am excited to be here.

Final Stage

She has a single good day, and then she seems worse. Several bad days come. The pendulum swings hard.

She has less and less to hang a thought on now.

To have this malady is to be robbed. Robbery is what makes Dementia go.

Now my mother rarely processes thought forms more complex than *I love you; how are you?* We traffic in emotions and facial expressions. I am in a Kabuki theater with my mother, one in which we are both playing down the situation.

There are things I want to talk with her about, but they're not in the scene. It's going on far longer than we want, but this is our play; this is our stage. The final stage.

I'm going to walk away at the end, and so is she. We'll leave through different doors.

You won't find anyone who looks like my mother on television. You won't find her shopping for tulips, cross-country skiing, riding a scooter through a resort, or laughing in the rain as she runs to her Jaguar. The old and ill and bedridden are locked out of media. They are erased as fast as their own memories are erased. But she exists. She is still beautiful. Suddenly, I want hair and makeup in here. I want Annie Leibovitz and a wind machine, and a man holding a light board. I want silk velvets to drape her in, and a ruby tiara and a ruby encrusted scepter to lay across her chest, like the Queen. I want to capture her simple majesty before the curtain falls.

Hard Facts

Here are some hard facts, the only two I know. It's a terrible illness, and I might have it, buried within me and about to bloom. I might also have cancer or a car accident. I could be hit by a car on my bike; I wear a helmet, but it's possible. Anything is possible. Like everything else in this life, I don't get to know.

But it is also a quixotic illness, and anything can happen.

Recently, in the middle of the night, my mother started talking very quietly and lucidly, and Ron took out his phone and recorded it for me. She mumbled to someone off camera, but then she faced forward, and she said some things very clearly.

She said that everything will be all right, and that we will all be all right, together. She called me Suz, though I was not there.

Then she said that she would call us back when she felt better. She said it in just the same way she always said it on our phone calls. It made me feel that there are layers to her and that some deeper layer is intact. In fact, I am going to take it as proof. It is proof.

And will that deep layer survive even death if it can live in the ravages of Dementia? I imagine her on the other side of this place, of this malady for which there is no cure, and she is free.

As I write this, a bird hits my bedroom window, lost. A moment later, it recovers and flies away.

Nadine and the Shamanic World

"I would much rather my mother was just immortal," I say in therapy.

"That would be best for all concerned," Nadine says.

She asks me about Abuelita. I tell her she was unmarried at twenty-two and considered an old maid. I tell her about the secret of Bunny and her adoption. I tell her how the history of Puerto Rico explains a lot about why the old ones keep so many secrets. They had to keep secrets to stay alive. They had to create instruments out of tin cans and houses out of abandoned Coca-Cola signs; there were complicated stories to tell and songs to be sung while hacking sugar cane with a dull blade and inhaling mouthfuls of flies all day long. They had to take their Santería religion underground and adopt the European saints as beards. They had to have dolls of rags and rich inner lives full of history and jokes and spirits. They had to invent cuisine out of yucca and plantain and rice and whatever roamed the island after the invaders came.

Nadine's eyes glitter.

"In the shamanic world," she says, "a lot of emphasis is placed on the ancestors. On healing the shame which was forced upon the ancestors..."

"But how?" I ask.

I am not leaving this Zoom until she tells me. I don't just want to heal myself, now. I want to heal my whole family.

"Walk into it," she says.

"Got it!" I say, and Zelle her payment.

Later, Dee and I were walking to dinner, both wearing long skirts and heels that clacked on the pavement. The nearby jasmine released its scent, and for a moment, I was back in school, and we were walking to a dance.

My time in Dementia has rubbed off on my regular life. It has thinned the veil between the worlds. I resolve to keep my eyes open for more portals.

The Brave Taino

She sits and stares at the Nature Channel, barefaced, her hair a wild nimbus. In the past, this would bother her, but her ego has fallen away, like the plain muslin wrapping off a crown.

What do I bring her now? It used to be jewelry, but now she looks at it blankly, as though I've handed her a wombat. What's fit to lay before her? Nothing. She wants nothing. The hardest gift of all. This is what it's like to die and to see clearly. She's there already. She is the brave Taino tribeswoman who has gone ahead of the others to report back.

My mother has a lesson for me: that objects are meaningless. Only food and love matter.

I know this is not the final lesson.

Sound Healing

Nadine has suggested more RSC. *Radical self-care.* What about a massage? Even better, what about a sound healing? I find a woman in Oakland though Yelp.

Natalie is a sound healer and a clairvoyant. As it happens, we both went to Berkeley Psychic Institute, or BPI as it's called. There were classes and seminars and an inspirational school song. A message already that this is not random. I decide it's an up level. I decide all of this is necessary.

"Take off your shoes and get on the table," she says.

I lie face up and fully clothed on the massage table, and she covers me with a blanket. A young woman with wide-set eyes, light brown hair, and an upbeat countenance.

Long sigh.

"This is for me," I say to the ceiling.

"I invite you to start to take a few deep breaths and gather your awareness and start to ground."

There are several giant Chinese gongs on the wall with gold markings on them and various percussion instruments. Elaborate tuning forks, which will soon be held by my ears and body pressure points and struck like a blow. This will feel good to me. As a child, I remember my mother cleaning out my ears, the exquisite pleasure. I'd lay my head on her lap, and she would clean them.

"My mother is a clairvoyant as well," I say.

"That's great," Natalie says. Nonplussed. As though I'd told her my mother was an accountant.

I explain to Natalie that Bunny's in her mid-eighties, and she has dementia and is in home hospice. I mention the memoir I'm writing.

"I can't wait to hear an interview with you and Terry Gross about it," Natalie says.

We laugh.

"Say your full name for me," Natalie says.

I say it.

"What do you want to look at?"

"My mother," I say. "The way she is dying."

A minute goes by.

"There's a lot of permission for things to not be perfect. And that's a match between the two of you. You are good at being the Witness. Your role is to allow her the space she needs to do what she's doing. And validating her on a crown chakra level. It's a crown-to-crown communication you have now."

I think of the old Imperial Margarine ad where a woman is crowned simply for choosing the correct spread for their toast. A bell would ring, and suddenly, she'd be bathed in golden light and crowned.

"I have to let go of the picture of the mother who is invincible. And allow her to have her end of life. This is her life," I say.

"I see how your mom as a spirit really called you in. You were the answer to her prayer."

I tell her about the dream Bunny had when she was pregnant. She said I came to her and said I wanted to be named Suzanne with a Z and Lynne with two Ns and an E. The way I spelled it out in the dream.

"I'm also just watching how much your mom wants to help you. How even when she crosses over, she is still going to help you."

"Oh, good," I say.

"Get back to basics," Natalie says, as she begins the sound bath. "Create new grounding for yourself and hook it up to the Supreme Being."

The gongs sound like musical thunder coming from far away. The precursor to rain. Singing bowls chime and reverberate, a small symphony. I breathe it in and release it, then pause. Something has gone through me and brushes me clean. A police siren from the street somehow blends perfectly. A Harley Davidson lumbers by. It's part of the symphony.

Now she is playing cymbals. How can she play all these instruments? I think of the Hindu goddess with eight arms.

After a long time, a tuning fork near my ears snaps me into the present moment. Then a tiny sharp bell.

Deep breaths as I come back to the room, as I float back up, a submarine that has been allowed to rise from the ocean floor.

My voice is different now. I sound stoned.

"Is my mother in this room now? Does she have a message for me?"

Any calls while I was out?

"I see her just pouring out so much gratitude for you."

"Is she all right?"

Now I sound five.

"Yes, she's okay. She's also showing me how hard you are on yourself. 'Tell her she doesn't have to be so hard on herself,' she's saying. 'Enjoy the small things in life.' She's showing me nature scenes."

"Is she showing you any timeline for her transition?" I ask.

"Not really."

"Yes. We feel like she doesn't have any plans to leave any-time soon."

Laughter.

Natalie looks out the small, shuttered window. There are big cracks where the light gets in.

"I'm showing Bunny that she has a lot more mobility than she thinks. This is in opposition to where she was told she was going to go. And it doesn't have to be a final decision. I'm watching her release other people's definitions of the other side that aren't her own."

"For a while she went to a void because it was quiet and peaceful. But now, she has turned around and is visiting others who have passed before her. Getting reacquainted. That might help her leave sooner."

I tell Natalie that she predicted she would die at eighty-one, and that's the year she was diagnosed.

"There's only a part of her here," Natalie says.

"I wonder what she's waiting for," I say.

"I wonder if she just really wanted to enjoy the death process," Natalie says.

"There are a lot of people here who still love her, so that may be tripping her up. There was a time when I wish she would pass. But I am over that now," I say.

"Say her full name for me," she says.

Which name? I think. *Which mother?*

"Olga Iris Irizarry is her birth name. Then she was adopted and became Bunny Nunez. Then Bunny Finnamore. And then she met the love of her life and became Bunny Mathews. Her professional name was Adrian."

A long minute passes as she processes the name roster.

"Well, she looks like she's having a great time as she wanders through time. She's dancing and winking at me. She wants to keep the option to come back even though she's already kind of left."

"I miss her knowing just what to say," I say. *I mean, I'm glad she's partying in the* Bardo, *but what about me? Insufferable me?*

"But she's laughing and saying, 'It's your turn, Suz,'" Natalie says.

This is, in fact, exactly what Bunny would say.

I get up. I feel lighter and more hopeful. I pay her.

As I leave, I sing the BPI song, and she joins in. We raise some sort of invisible metaphysical chalice and clink with one another.

My Mother's Voice

I want to never balk. I want to be like Ram Dass, who tended his dying father without flinching, even though he called him Rum Dum. Ram Dass, who said that the game is to be where you are, as honestly and as consciously as you know how. To do things not as though they are a great burden but just part of the dance.

"Well. Ram Dass had a lot of help" is what Bunny would have said. "He had *people*."

She says it now, inside my mind, and I see her in a seventies updo and an orange poncho pantsuit, standing next to her birth father Felipe in the late seventies. Felipe, my maternal grandfather who never once approached me. A man without whose help, my mother would certainly not have lived to come from Puerto Rico. Felipe, a man both false and true. Like my own father. Like everyone.

She is there, always. My mother's voice, her true voice. I can't remember the last truly lucid conversation with her. It is the same for my father. Parents, it seems, are what I misplace.

I want my mother to be delivered from where she is in Dementia. I want her to have Quality of Life, that elusive butterfly. But this is her life. As in all things, I can accept, or I can suffer. It's time to grow up. This is the deadline. It's the absolute final deadline when our mothers move on. It's what Bunny used to call *the drop deadline*.

All About Purgatory

I am reading *A Widow's Story* by Joyce Carol Oates. Her longtime husband died, and she went on; in fact, she straightaway remarried one of her husband's doctors. This is something I consider sensible and wise and which angered a lot of people who wished her more suffering.

And now I know her late husband. Like Tom, Raymond Green was Catholic. He believed that venal sins send you to Purgatory and mortal sins send you to Hell. The Church teaches that you can work your way out of Purgatory eventually; you can do it in steps. Your family can help you by praying to the Virgin Mary for intercession with God; they can pay for masses to be said in your name and for the redemption of your soul. To be prayed over after your death is a kind of lobbying, Oates says. It is possible to ease the dead into Paradise through the back door, thus the Hail Mary pass, the one that wins many a football game at the last minute.

Purgatory is life as a prison sentence from which one might be redeemed, Oates writes. But once you are in Hell, you're there. Torments forever.

Yet Hell was vivid and overseen by the devil, who you just know is a lot of fun. In Hell, you had a personal devil that tortured you exclusively. It seemed, I thought, a lot livelier than Purgatory.

I yawn. I turn a page. I read some more. Joyce was a mess. She makes me feel less alone. I touch the smooth back cover of the book. Joyce Carol Oates looks radiant.

Falling Through the Holes

Today, she doesn't know me at all. Not when I try, and not when I try harder. Not when I arrive, and not when I leave. Today, I fell through the holes in her brain.

Dementia and its treacherous, lacy holes, crocheted by the gods of malevolence, have pushed me outside the womb for good.

It's time.

You come into a room through a door, the only possible door. Take away the door you came through. Take away your mother.

Now you're alone. Where to go from here?

You must leave through a window. Climb to the roof of the house. Jump or stay put, it matters not. This is the time of mourning. It lasts forever. Appreciate the quality of the house you've been brought to, of the roof. Address the stars.

Memento Mori

I tell Nadine that being with my mom in Dementia, with its attendant and constant awareness of active dying, is jarring, as though I'm standing on the lip of oblivion every day.

"What's wrong with actively dying?" Nadine says. "We all are."

She's right. I pay her.

Muriel Spark wrote that without an ever-present sense of death, life is insipid. That you may as well live on the whites of eggs. She said that death, when it approaches, ought not to take one by surprise. That being aware of it was the best way to enrich your existence. She advised that women be alert to recognize the prime of their life, whenever it may occur.

Later, as I am folding and putting away laundry, I am thinking *Hi Ho, Hi Ho, it's off to Death we go...*

I do a little soft shoe in the hallway in my socks. I move my feet and sway, arms overhead. What the Hell, in other words.

There's a homemade sign on the off-ramp to my house that says "Everything will be okay," on Highway 13 at Park Boulevard. It has a wreath of twigs and dried flowers affixed next to it; it's yellow and made of tin. It has been there ever since I moved back to Oakland four years ago. They color the letters in when they fade; they keep the sign alive through all seasons. Who is doing this? God in drag, Ram Dass would say.

I know it won't be okay, and I know it will be okay. We are all on the celestial teeter totter, and no one is getting out of this intact.

But this sign is suggestive of a higher truth, and I roll down my window, and I touch it before the light turns green again, before I have to move forward. I think of how I am touching the person who tends to the sign. I am touching grace.

Revelations

I lose my driver license—something that's never happened. All day, I look everywhere, heart pounding, muttering insults to myself. I call around. I tell myself I know the numbers, have memorized the numbers. I imagine reciting them to a policeman and him frowning and asking me to step out of the vehicle.

The next day, I simply drive without it. Everything, I see now, is not vital.

Unassailable

"How are you? Are you okay?" My mother asks me this morning.

This stuns me.

"I'm okay, yes," I say.

"You've got to feel good about yourself," she says.

And she does. I can see it in her face: the way she has always been essentially unassailable. Dementia has no purchase in this moment. It can sod right off.

You must understand. Dementia is where my mother lives, but it is not who she is. Her eyes are hers. Her spirit is still elegant. If she doesn't hear you, she'll say, "I beg your pardon?"

Somewhere inside lies a sacred core, untouched. An essence patrolled by sentinels of light. And if that's true for her, it's true for everyone.

Dementia isn't the defining chapter of her life. Hiroshima was not the pinnacle of Japan.

Today, I shave my mother. Her skin is a brown riverbed, fissured and soft. She has the beginnings of a fine beard. A Van Dyke. But no.

I shave her gently with olive oil. Her head has shrunk. There is less to shave. I try to hurry. She has strict boundaries now. She viciously guards what is left.

I never imagined this task, but it isn't bad. There are instant results. Something is cleaned, something is banished. We get to be very close. She forgets right away that I have crossed her.

What Else She Forgets

She forgets that she is bedridden. She forgets that her son is gone. She forgets the full life she used to have and no longer has. She forgets those who betrayed her. She forgets being hungry. She forgets the mother she never knew. She forgets her birth father, who passed on her and sashayed down the streets of the Lower East Side, tilting his new fedora. She forgets the housing projects. She forgets the husband who left. She forgets her hysterectomy, her two long labors, her knee replacements. She forgets her abortion. She forgets getting old. She forgets collapsing and breaking her legs.

She remembers her people. She remembers Central Park.

It is an ill wind that blows nobody any good. Here in Dementia, all the clichés come crackling into life.

Marathon

Winter has slammed down like a dark shade over what was already dark. Soon we go into year three of the pandemic and year five in Dementia with my mother.

Nadine says it is a marathon.

169

"An ultra-marathon," she says. Professionally upgrading the tornado.

"How do I deal with it?" I ask.

"One foot in front of the other," she says.

I wait for more. I need more.

"Take all the water they give you."

A Dream of Walking

Last night, I dreamt my mother was walking normally and wore pink capri pants. I was overjoyed. *How did it happen?* I asked Ron in the dream.

He had taken her for a drive, and she had simply forgotten she couldn't walk. When they got home, she was walking room to room and wearing a low kitten heel in black. Her hair was in a puffy updo. I was showing her around her house, showing her the places I had cleaned and organized.

I think of the Lakota prayer in *Black Elk Speaks*.

> With visible breath I am walking.
> A voice I am sending as I walk.
> In a sacred manner I am walking.

I believe she is transitioning. One foot here and one foot there.

Discovery

Nadine suggests I share on social media about my mom's predicament. That raising awareness would also raise my awareness. She has seen it happen, she says.

Every day, I write a dispatch, and I think *I can't post this*, and then I post it. I am surprised by the number of strangers and friends who know about Dementia, fellow travelers. I am not alone.

Now I see that the country we live in and the boundaries of Dementia are separate, but they also overlap. As I speak to other people like me, I see the extent of the overlap. I see that dementia is not an isolated part of life; it is life. My mother lives in Dementia, but she is also still in life. When I visit, I am in both worlds. We are all, I see, dual citizens. We share a greater landscape.

Resurrection

I find a picture in my mother's things, a baby in an elaborate wicker stroller, posed with a pacifier in his mouth. This picture belonged to my grandma Sarah, the woman who adopted my mom. Sarah, who as a small child I thought was Aunt Bea on *Leave it to Beaver* because she looked just like her, the brown version. On the back is inscribed, "In Remembrance to his mother, Sarah Nunez. Born the 18th of March, 1929."

I look at it again and again. It has to be what it is. Sarah's baby. Although we were told, my mother was told, that she could never have children.

This is a secret baby, hidden in hundreds of old photographs. A baby who died and was never spoken of. The one who came before my mother came across the sea on the Borinquen to heal the hole.

I don't believe my mother knew. We were close; she would have told me.

When Boricua want to keep a secret, they keep it. My mother was with Sarah when she died. Nothing.

In the picture, he is fat, robust. He is looking at the camera with a gimlet eye. *What took you so long*, he seems to be asking.

He has a name. It is Ferdinand Nunez, Jr. Fred for short.

I say it aloud, and for a moment, he lives. He rises from beneath the ground in which he was buried in New York, 1929. Takes his place among his people. Dances.

When I was four, my parents made me go to Vacation Bible School, and I woke up and began to panic. I went looking for my grandma's cabin because I was scared. But as soon as I got on the path, I looked up, and she was walking toward me.

This tells you everything you need to know about Sarah.

Mashed Potatoes

We were exposed to COVID-19 again. But I FaceTime. Ron holds up his iPad, and she touches the screen where my face is, her face full of wonder. And it is wonderful. I feel this every time. A miracle that came just in time for the pandemic.

I describe the Thanksgiving dinner I am bringing on Saturday. There's no response until I get to the mashed potatoes when her eyes light up.

"All right!" she says.

Mashed potatoes have great power and may illicit a response from anywhere in Dementia.

"Last night she woke up and started calmly speaking in a voice I hadn't heard," Ron tells me.

Not a voice he hadn't heard but one he had given up hearing again.

"She assured me that she was all right and *would be all right*. It lasted less than a minute, but it comforted me."

I take this piece of light and run.

Winter Solstice

It's the winter solstice. The longest night is upon us, the shortest day.

I fill the bird feeder. A sparrow arrives, bustling onto the perch. He was waiting for this. What I do matters. The smallest arc transcribes.

A train in the distance. The hum of the clothes dryer. A little dog, snoring at my feet. There is a play going on here. The train blows its horn again, the sound curling up to me.

I want to get on the train, let it take me somewhere brighter than this day. Take me away from where my mother journeys in Dementia, lost but for a few breadcrumbs of memory. But I also fear the train. I am too old for flight for its own sake. I know what follows.

Another bird comes, bullying the first away. The 11:03 calls, farther on now. The silence it leaves behind is softened. I've made a choice.

The dog jumps up. A delivery arrives, a gift from a stranger. The light, already beginning to grow.

Mountain View Cemetery

It's Christmas, and we are driving Tom's kids around Oakland. They are visiting from their mom's house on the east coast.

As we pass the Chapel of the Chimes Funeral Home, I am wondering if we will be there soon with my mother. Across the street are the sweeping grounds of Mountain View Cemetery.

The rolling hills canting to one side have a Walt Disney appeal, speckled with little mausoleum houses and tombs, marble statues of nymphs and dogs and a plethora of angels. At the entrance are giant, lighted holiday Santa and His Sleigh figures circling the drive. There are tall wooden soldier Nutcracker figures with faux fur hats. Here, death is a Winter Wonderland. It seems like death could be a ride, in fact.

We all go for ice cream at Fenton's. I order the large milkshake with caramel sauce. I am done ordering the small milkshake without caramel sauce. That time, of deliberating and measuring and limiting and restricting and preening, is over.

The Train

My mother cherished my brother's and my childhood. She'd call, wistful, to say, "Last night I dreamt you were little again…"

I felt slighted. Was I not supposed to grow up?

Year by year, she grew more childlike, more dependent on Ron. I thought she was giving up. Taking the easy path.

I didn't know she was speeding along on the train to Dementia, away from us.

I didn't know that my favorite dream, the one I've never had, is the one where Pablo is a baby, and I feel his toothless, gummy mouth cupping my chin.

I didn't know that even hurtling away, brain bleeding and legs wizened, she was stronger than I would ever be.

Comfort Sound

I listen to the same books on Audible, familiar and dear. I listen to *The Prince of Tides*, again and again. Again and again, Tom Wingo releases the gas station tiger to eat the rapists that have escaped from the local asylum. Again and again, he dangles the Stradivarius out the penthouse window of his therapist who is also his lover. I listen to *Terms of Endearment* on a perpetual loop. Aurora Greenway and her maid Rosie argue repeatedly. Royce drives his potato chip truck onto the dance floor again and again.

I listen to *The Four Agreements*, *The Fifth Agreement*, Wayne Dyer seminars, *The Untethered Soul*, *Loving What Is* by Byron Katie. I listen to widow memoirs. *The Year of Magical Thinking*. *A Widow's Story*. *What Comes Next and How to Like It* by Abigail Thomas, as well as *A Three Dog Life*, which is about her husband, Rich, who died chasing after their beagle, Harry, who lived. I feel Abigail Thomas knows about complex loss and can lead me out. Tom and I went to see her speak in Raleigh, and we struck up a friendship.

I am soothed by magicians of ink, by the masters of words. I drift off this way, vectored to the past and headed to morning.

The Trouble Is

Abigail Thomas says that the moment I realize I have to stop dragging my mother to where I am is a big deal.

"I remember when I stopped trying to drag Rich into reality, and the rest of our times were somewhat easier, but often terribly sad. And even then, he would startle me with a strikingly pertinent remark, then disappear again."

"Does writing make it easier?" Abby asks me. "Something about this process might be useful. As my daughter-in-law said after she began writing about her stillborn son, 'writing makes a home for him.'"

I tell her if I get the same diagnosis, I will find a way to exit. Step off a cliff. Eat pills.

"I plan to off myself too if I know this is coming," she says. "The trouble is that I might leave it too long and forget."

Abigail Thomas says we should all have a sandwich board that says SORRY on one side and GO FUCK YOURSELF on the other side.

Always a good idea, she says. *Cover your emotional truth bases.*

I used just such a sandwich board during my divorce.

Abby knows all. The rest of us only guess.

I've been doing that thing where I go into the spare bedroom and smell Pablo's favorite quilt at the foot of his old twin trundle bed. And it smells like him as a child; it really and truly does. It has an indelible scent. I resolve to seal it in a plastic bag so it doesn't lose its scent.

I'm not sad. It's something more than sad and less than sad. I want him to be gone, and I want him to be here. The two can exist side by side.

I have a few of his onesies. His wrist rattle. I saved one of his bottles with Sylvester the Cat on it, both the bottle and the rubber nipple. Two pacifiers. The hospital nametag from his newborn ankle, the circumference of a quarter. My hospital wristband and Mark's wristband, which are connected to each other, as we are, by a kind of invisible tape.

The Mofongo Report

We ordered Puerto Rican food on Door Dash. There was great joy and bitter disappointment. The Lobster mofongo was far too chunky. You cannot trust a chunky mofongo. Where there are chunks, there is dryness.

The pernil (slow roasted pork shoulder) (Saturdays only) and the *arroz con gandules* were cruel perfection, as were the *tostones*, very light and crispy. But there were no maduros on the side. That felt wrong and even punitive. They always served a side of sweet maduros before. So, we got the green plantain tostones but not the ripe plantain maduros. There was plantain inequity.

The lobster itself was plentiful, but there was no real sauce bridge between the lobster and the mofongo. There were *camarón*, and those were good but again—no cohesiveness on the sauce front. And the mofongo was heavy: a hippopotamus versus a swan.

I cannot tell you what a bad mofongo does to you. There is a corollary here with bad matzo ball soup, which does not heal a cold; it worsens it. It makes a head cold seem the least of your problems. But with bad matzo ball soup, refuge can be taken in the rich chicken stock. Whereas bad mofongo is much, much worse than no mofongo at all. Like love, mofongo cannot be compromised. Once you have, it's finished.

Stay

She has survived hospitalization twice. She has serenely triumphed over the plague, not giving it a single thought. She has no bed sores or respiratory kerfuffle. Pneumonia has not come to call. She has not died, and in fact is on track to live forever, a café au lait Methuselah.

Yesterday, she greeted me like my mother. She asked how I was. She recognized almost everyone on the Parade of Faces. I brought her a Christmas tin of chocolate hollow snowmen. She put one in her mouth and started to eat it without removing the wrapper. A minor glitch. I removed the thin foil, and she ate its head.

The terrain in Dementia runs inexorably and swiftly down-hill, but for my mother, this only seems to make her hair fly behind her like a commemorative flag. She remains largely cheerful, herself. I take notes for my own demise. This is how it's done.

Orange Poncho Pantsuit

I am on the bed next to Bunny while Tom is cleaning the gutters. I'm watching the Parade of Faces with her. Some days, she says almost nothing. I don't know what kind of day this is, but I cast out a line.

"So, I sold another book to be published, Mommy..."

"All right!" she says.

"It's about you."

"Oh, no."

We laugh.

"No, it's good. It's all the good things. I didn't put it any of the hard things, Mommy. It's about your magical life and all the ordinary magic you made happen. And it's about all the Puerto Ricans in our family. Grandma Sarah is in it and Abuelita and Pinkie and Felipe, except he doesn't come off so good."

She says nothing. She's done with grudges. She is teaching me, as always.

"You know how you wanted me to write a book about your family?"

"Yes."

"Well, now I have, and it's going to be published at the end of this year. So, I may dedicate it to you, okay?"

"Aw, thank you, darling."

"Do you want me to say *To Bunny* in the dedication?"

"That's up to you."

"Is he cute?" Mom says. She is turning her attention back to the Parade of Faces. A picture of Pablo as a toddler in a bubble bath.

"Yes, he's your grandson. He's very cute," I say.

"I love this picture, Mommy..." I say.

It's Bunny standing next to her biological father Felipe, wearing an orange poncho bell bottom pantsuit, trimmed with white pom poms. Her hair is in a black bouffant; her eyeliner is perfect.

"You always had such style," I say.

"She's one of a kind," Ron says admiringly. He has wandered in.

"I've been telling her what a wonderful mother she has been my whole life and how lucky I am to have her. Look at her. She's a doll of life," I say to Ron.

Now the Parade of Faces shows Bunny in a white fur hooded coat in Manhattan, age three, surrounded by dolls. Her adoptive parents are lavishing her with gifts. She has been plucked from the hammock of death in Mayaguez, where Leonor would leave her when she went off looking for food. She has been wholly resurrected. But her eyes are wary.

"Where's your husband?" Bunny says.

"He's on the roof."

"Why is he on the roof?"

"Because the gutters are full of leaves. He'll come in and see you pretty soon," I say.

My mother thinks Tom is handsome, and she perks up whenever he arrives. She doesn't always recognize him, but she recognizes game.

"So, Richard is in it. My Dad's in it. Do you remember Richard, Mommy?"

"I had another husband?"

"You did. You had another husband."

"Who?"

"His name was Richard Finnamore."

"Oh yeah. What happened to him?" she says. Casual.

"He died. He wore out really fast, Mommy. He died when I was nineteen, and his wife died with him. What the fuck was that about?" I say.

The accident has never ceased to amaze me.

There's a picture of my mom in high school.

"Look at how beautiful you were, Mommy."

"Yeah, that was nice," Bunny says. A picnic she went to once.

"There's your son," I say, as a picture of my brother at one of his piano recitals appears.

"Do you love him?" I ask.

"Yeah, I sure do."

"He loves you too, Mommy," I say.

He loves you so much that he can't bear to see you like this. Or else he loves you so little that he needn't trouble himself to see you like this. Which is it? We don't get to know. I will err on the side of mercy.

"There's my husband!" I say. A picture of Tom doing yard work.

"He is a sweet man," Mom says. She remembers him in this moment. I try not to cling to this unexpected joy. This whole conversation is a miracle on the level of stigmata.

In the next picture, Sarah is standing in front of her house with big black glasses on. The light had begun to torment my grandmother as she approached the age of one hundred. "That was just before she passed," I say.

"She died?" Bunny says, aghast.

We breeze by this. Every moment the Etch A Sketch in her brain allows for these smooth transitions.

"Are you going to live to be very old, Mommy?"

"No!"

"You're already eighty-seven," I point out.

"OH, GOD," she says, making a comic face.

"There's me and Dee. She's still my best friend," I confide. "Do you remember Dee?"

Like Anderson Cooper, I am asking all the hard questions.

"No."

Undeterred, I point to the front sunroom, which is now closed off.

"Do you remember you'd see all your clients in that room?"

"Yes." Laughs.

"You had a pretty good business going, Mommy."

Mmmmm. She says. Pass, in other words. *Next question.*

"What do you think happens when we die Mommy? Do we go to heaven, or do we get reborn again?"

"Could be both," Bunny says after considering for a moment.

"There's grandma Sarah's baby that died," I say, seeing the one surviving photograph of him in an antique wicker stroller.

"Grandma had some good secrets," I say.

My mother nods.

"All your family seem to have a lot of secrets. I guess they just had to because times were so hard on the island."

My mother nods.

"I'm letting all the secrets out now," I say.

"Good," Bunny says.

The Hard Things

My mother was agoraphobic for much of her adult life. When we went somewhere, she had to sit in the exit row so that she could leave early. She suffered from clinical depression after her hysterectomy. Throughout my twenties, I had to leave work and go sit with her while Ron was at work. She could not go shopping with me or see friends with me like the other mothers could. We traveled together a few times, and she fueled herself with courage and a big Scotch at night, although ordinarily she never drank. After menopause, she gained weight and became obese, as she was only five feet tall. All of these things—the weight gain, the depression—may have helped her along the road to Dementia. They may have been the wheels on her feet that sped her there. I don't get to know.

But here she is. Splendid, deeply flawed: Estate jewelry versus new gold.

She is still broadcasting, my mother, only with less bandwidth. I hear her broken yet familiar song and hum along. It is my privilege.

Penultimate Lesson

My mother's penultimate lesson? Remain yourself for as long as you can. Despite disease or a collection of syndromes. Remain your best self.

Remember who you are, she used to say to me when I was troubled.

But who am I now without her supreme intellect and advice?

Looking in the mirror, I see her eyebrows, one cocked, one not. I see her eyes, her mouth. An expression of ineffable surprise. I am her, I see, just less cooked.

Pablo and the Soul

My mother is losing her ability to hold a fork.

"The soul doesn't age at least," Pablo says to me when I tell him this on the phone. He is working at the seafood counter at his supermarket job, but it's slow.

"If you're alive today, that's still a miraculous anomaly," he says.

"Thank you," I say.

"I've been doing some thinking about age—almost all the customers here are older—and having passed childhood, it no longer seems like a stretch to reach that point before I know it. So, I've been letting go of that feeling you have when you're very young, that older people are especially different. I have to go now, Mama."

He hangs up because even though it's late at night, someone is awake, and he has to sell them King Salmon for thirty dollars a pound.

When he calls me *Mama*, I know he is especially pleased. When he calls me *Mom*, I know he is just normal. When he calls me *Suzanne*, I know he is furious.

I admire that he already sees that it's not simple but quick to go from twenty to ninety. This knowledge will serve him well.

I feel a bit better and order food from La Perla to celebrate.

Delivered or eaten there, La Perla is in the sacred circle of trust. You can't see it from the street; you have to know it's there, like a magical castle. It's in the back of a liquor store near Fruitvale in Oakland. We order some food almost every Saturday. They only serve pernil on Saturdays because it takes two days to roast the pork shoulder until it falls off in tender strips of delicacy. The portions are large, and the arroz con gandules and the fried tostones are ridiculous.

What do they put in their secret sauce that comes in the world's tiniest cup? I make a mental note to ask. I dip the tostone in the sauce. Tostones are small, pretzel-shaped plantains or yucca that are pounded with a mortar and pestle with fresh garlic and herb slivers, then formed into an orb and quickly deep fried and then dipped warm into the sauce in a paper thimble. And I feel better. I really, really do.

When in doubt, get a large rice with red beans, and have some Piri Piri sauce on that on another day, with maybe some roast chicken. Medium Piri Piri. If you frequently visit loved ones in the country of Dementia, do not wait for other people to heal you. Heal yourself.

The Lost Crown

I place a stick of gum in my mouth, and it sucks loose a ceramic crown from my lower left molar as easily as butter sliding off a knife. I stop everything, aware that where there was once a sugary pleasant wad, there is now what feels like an enormous hard glass ball thinly wrapped in gum. I am aware that if I chew even once more, I can have the sensation of breaking one tooth with another tooth, of chewing on my own teeth.

The crown is still in my coin purse. I went to the dentist yesterday, and he said, *Implant.* He said, *That molar won't hold a crown.* I was skeptical. He showed me an X-ray of that area. I believe now. It was like looking into a sinkhole in Calcutta.

An implant begins with an extraction. Then they do a bone graft, which hurts like a small amputation. Then they wait six months to *see* if the bone has grafted. Then they take a special X-ray that costs three hundred dollars. Then, if enough bone has been successfully grafted, they screw in a screw. An actual screw. Then they put a post around that. Then they add a temporary crown. Then they go to the lab and fashion a porcelain crown. It all costs seven thousand dollars.

But that implant will never fail you or leave you—long after death it will hold steady. I can chew things even after I'm dead. But it's seven thousand dollars, so I can't have one. But I have other molars.

Do I really a need a tooth there? I decide I do not. My mother has lost a molar this year, and so I can be in solidarity with her now. What I also see is that this is how it goes. Losing parts of yourself so you can travel light. Still, I feel teeth were one of God's mistakes. Maybe his biggest.

Nadine says that the Navajo weave a mistake into every blanket, and also something else. They call it the spirit line or the weaver's path—a small line that runs horizontally to the edge of the rug. They don't want to have their soul trapped inside the weaving and need a way to exit through the spirit line. I like the idea of this. It speaks to an eventual truth, which is that we all need a way out, and that we need to be the ones to plan it.

In the Navajo nation, mistakes are handled purposely, perfection is not a goal. These weavings take a long time to learn. It takes six months to weave a textile. So, they're not going to make a mistake unless they want to make a mistake.

I fervently hope that God is like this.

Target

Dee and I go to Target. I've persuaded her to get the Red Card so that every purchase is 5 percent off. Every single one. When Target sends me a notification about a sale on boots, I send her the link. Recently, I found black and brown leather boots lined with faux shearling, $24.99, after a flash sale of 30 percent off. A perfect, low heel. I alerted her at once, and we both bought them in both colors. She is an eight and a half, and I am a nine. She can wear my shoes, but I can't wear hers.

Target is an island of sanity in an uncertain time with popcorn and a coffee bar and individual Pizza Hut pizzas. We visit often, sometimes electronically and sometimes in real life. Today we are at her Target in Chico. We note how different Targets have different things. When she comes down to Oakland, we will go to my Target.

As we walk down the brightly-lit aisles, we breathe in the rich retail air. We marvel at the low prices. We are each on a quest to buy our third purchase in thirty days of thirty-five dollars to obtain a twenty dollar gift card. She finds bath salts and candles, and I find a pink cardigan and mashed potatoes. In Target, as in life, we share a single cart.

Nadine and the Approach to Death

I tell Nadine that it is better now that Bunny's in hospice at home. That the Chaplain, a very nice man named Phil, came and asked Ron if Bunny had any religion, and Ron said, *She was a clairvoyant.* Which seemed to wrap the conversation up.

"Hospice sets you free," Nadine agrees, "because it represents support. It formalizes the fact of an approaching death."

Nadine is certified in end-of-life care. She has watched and helped hundreds of people die. She is an honorary Angel of Death.

"So when Bunny takes her last breath, you won't be surprised. You will be shocked."

"Because she's been here," I say in agreement. "Even though she's in Dementia, she's still here. I walk in, she says, 'Hi, honey.'"

"Still here, yes. When you're sharing air, you're sharing air. When she stops breathing, it's final. He was dying for months, but when my husband Mark took his last breath, it was a shock. Not a surprise. So, when people say, *Well, didn't you know it was coming?* They don't get it. Or, *Isn't she better off? She's not suffering!* They don't get it," Nadine says.

I confess to Nadine that I really miss the Suzanne that could just frolic. I'm finding myself not booking vacations. It doesn't feel right now.

Nadine throws up both hands. She has had it with me.

"So that's our point of focus in truth. You have a mom with final stage dementia. It's not her fault. It was in her bloodline and who knows where else. But you have the right to step away and be thankful when there's something good happening. Yet the mind doesn't want to give you that because the mind is contentious. Why? I can't tell you. We may go a few minutes over if that's okay with you..."

Show me a therapist who isn't watching the clock, and I will show you a healer.

"You may not be able to see beauty and hope until your mom dies. Because even though you know that she's in good hands with hospice, totally loved by Ron and by you and cared for, there's still a process going on every day of your life that she is declining. But you have the honor of being able to spend time with her rather than getting a phone call from the police that your mother dropped dead."

BOOM.

"Part of you is constantly with your mom. You don't have full capacity to get regulated with everyone else. You're juggling realities. So, you hear some good news, and in the moment, it's fabulous. And then the mind starts in...*What about next year? What about next month? What about this? What about that?* That's when you tell your mind time out, *fuck off.* I'm going to stay focused on the present moment because I don't know what's coming later."

Did Nadine just say fuck? Because I am here for it.

"You're witnessing the process of the departure of your mother—body, mind, spirit. Your work is to observe, to recognize that you're in the midst of the truth of what life is. And your mind is troubled holding so much space. And so, you say to Tom, 'You know what? I can't sit on a beach and pretend I'm having a vacation.'"

"Yes," I say. "Because it would be pretending. Plus, it would interrupt our rituals. He comes home from work; I make him dinner, and we watch HBO. Is that also pretending? I honestly don't know. I'll be sitting next to him, and we're having chips and dip, and I'm thinking, *Wow, I'm really a bit depressed, and I'm worried.* But I don't say that to him."

"Right," Nadine says. "Because he can't do anything with it. And it seems to also give more power to the worry. Because you're verbalizing it. It's a double-edged sword—sometimes it helps, and other times it perpetuates more things to worry about, and it drags the other person in."

I think of being in a pit of tigers and reaching out to snake a hand around Tom's ankle. I think about crabs in a bucket.

"Rituals help," Nadine says. "You might plant a tree in your yard, and every day you water it, loving Bunny by creating life on the earth. It puts some form to the intention to honor the best possible sense of wellbeing, even amid chaos. When I was teaching my staff at the spa in Punto del Este in Uruguay, I told them, 'We're not looking to cure anybody. We're looking to bring the loving touch of our hands to their body, for balance and to be there for them, to give them the gift of presence.'"

"You're being asked not only to be her biological daughter, but to be her godmother. You're being asked to see her from a different perspective and dimension."

Yes. The dimension of Dementia I am traversing. The travel log I write in daily. How does Nadine know? And how will I get her permission to write about her teachings once more, as I did in *Split*? But I know it will happen. That it has, in some way, already happened. This is the power of Nadine.

"You're being challenged to hold it in a different place in your psychic system. And when that truly can shift for you, that's when you look at Tom and say, I'm ready for vacation. And it can shift because you deserve it, and he deserves it."

"So for now, whether it's going to yoga class, whether it's doing some pottery, some clay work, or grabbing some water colors and doing whatever kind of expressive therapeutic act, it's your homework to release whatever you're holding that actually is cluttering the psychic space between you and Tom and you and your mom. This may mean starting off with an Epsom salt bath and rosemary or Roman chamomile and lavender. Something that is saying, I'm taking care of me in honor of them. Your mom cannot get up and take a bath on her own."

On Saturdays, she used the little round bath gels from Avon and the Calgon bath beads. She'd take off her polyester leopard print jumpsuit and her small kitten heels and Calgon would take her the fuck away. She would give herself what she would call an Overhaul: bubble bath, wash and condition her hair, shave her legs. She'd tweeze her brows in her lighted makeup mirror with vanity table that Ron built into their closet. Completely rapt, I would watch her, a black-haired movie star in a closet.

Nadine rings the singing bowl.

"Bunny is imparting information to you that you are meant to glean and integrate for her and for everybody you've ever known or loved."

The next day, I recite my sankalpa. *My mother is on her path.* And I am back inside my own body. My mind isn't twisting my innards and squirting black ink into my eyes to blind me with dread. I book us for an overnight on Tom's birthday.

And every so often, little unexplained updrafts of joy rise from my toes to the top of my head, shooting like a tiny comet skyward.

Calistoga

It's Tom's birthday, and we are spending a night in the wine country. On the way to Calistoga, we pass the gazebo in the park where my father and his third wife Gayle were married. We pass the old Bonita Motel where the wedding party stayed. I remember Gayle with curlers in her black hair, her chocolate Aztec eyes full of joy and determination. In two years, she would be gone, dead on a Shasta highway with her new husband. Her mind will never fade, her beauty will abide.

At lunch, our table was laid for three versus two, and I thought, *Dad.*

Rain was forecasted, but it only came at night. During the day the skies were full of both clouds and sun; the light would change every second or so, illuminating the yellow and pink leaves of fall. It was like being inside God's camera. Later it was sprinkling while the sun was out. This seemed to echo my mood. Two things at once, dark and light. In America when this happens, *the devil is beating his wife.* In Puerto Rico, they would say, *Witches are getting married.*

In the mineral pool, it was foggy, but every so often the clouds would part, and the full moon would emerge, a creamy white orb. Each time we saw it was a gift we opened together; my legs wrapped around Tom's as we clung to a single floatation noodle.

There is a wicker Judas gate outside the lodge house where we slept in the decorative fountain. A Judas gate is a small door located in a larger door so that a person can enter quietly. There is a Victorian painting by Tissot which shows just such a gate, in which Judas is seen stepping through on his way to betray Christ in the garden. In many ways, the Judas gate is the one I walk through when I go to see my mom, and it's the one I use when I leave her, guilty but with a frisson of relief. When I pass through it, I feel lighter and younger and freer having escaped the boundary of Dementia.

On the way home, we stop at the Napa Valley Olive Oil Company, the small, hidden olive oil store in a barn in St. Helena, where they have been hand-making olive oil for a hundred years. I buy two one-gallon jugs of olive oil, green and thick and pure. I will give one to Ron.

Inside it is dark, and I can see the track the old press moved along, can feel it underfoot, a guide.

I find what I need, and then I hear a woman say to the owner, "What's your name again?"

"Leonor."

And I get that feeling. The feeling that brujeria is in play, that my life is a play, staged with exquisite precision by a great unknown force. When the other woman leaves, I move into frame.

"Leonor. A name one rarely hears anymore," I say. "It's beautiful."

She agrees that it is.

"That was my grandmother's name," I say, the first time in my life I have acknowledged her as such.

As I walk to the car, I carry the gallons easily, one on each hooked forefinger.

In my mind, I am setting a place for Leonor as well. Let all the dead come to me.

Lucky

I had my waitress dream. My section is full, and I can't get to the bread station. Later I'm standing in front of my high school locker, and I realize again that I have forgotten the combination.

What is the cure, I ask myself. *What is the cure for life?*

I am not sure, but I pour myself a bowl of Lucky Charms, the cereal my grandma Sarah used to buy for me. We never had money for the sugary cereals at our house, but Sarah put some aside for Lucky Charms. I see where they have added many more marshmallow bits. It used to be just stars and moons, but now there are unicorns and shooting stars and purple horse-shoes. So, these now are even luckier than before.

I used to feel lucky because of certain things. Going to Berkeley, and getting in when the tuition was cheap. Having a son. Being almost tall. All kinds of random luck. Then when this happened to my mom, it felt as though my luck had worn out. But it has happened before. When my husband left me. When I went bankrupt. When my right hip crumbled.

Maybe luck is always there, like oxygen, and we just get used to it.

Now I feel lucky because she is bedridden and hasn't needed to be chased down the street naked and singing "Bésame Mucho." That Ron is with her still. That I still have Tom, whose last name is Luckenbach, surely a sign. There is also a sense that if I listed all the lucky things, it would never end.

Church

I go to Saint Andrew. I sing; I confess. I receive the healing.

Across the road from Saint Andrew is a Target. I consider the after-church trip to Target a sacrament. I buy our Thanksgiving turkey with Brussel sprouts and Hawaiian rolls. I use my "Buy $60 in groceries Get $15 off" promotional coupon. Halleluiah.

The day after Thanksgiving we deliver a meal to my parents' house. Roast turkey along with my mother's stuffing recipe, mashed potatoes, gravy, pumpkin pie. The works. When I was cooking yesterday, I consulted her recipe in my recipe card file and saw that it was in tatters, so I transcribed it. I like to think of my stepdaughter Faye making this recipe in the future.

She is tall and blonde and twenty, so she has no use for recipes now. She is the recipe.

What is there to buy on Black Friday? Nothing. We are in our sixties; we have everything. There should be a Black Friday van that will come to a house and divest it of everything that was bought on previous Black Fridays. It should be a community service.

At their double wide mobile home, I do what I always do. The dishes, the laundry, the vacuuming. The cat litter box. I help Ron change his sheets, even though he says it can wait. I need him sleeping on fresh sheets. When I was sick, my mother would change my sheets. She would sweep into the sick room with the majesty of a barrister and make change happen. I do this now when I am low. I change our sheets and fluff the pillows hard, thinking it will change the mood. Sometimes it does.

By unspoken agreement, I tackle the inside of my parent's house, and Tom does the outside. He stealthily throws away things from the back deck and from the outer fringes of the house. He gathers the empty plastic milk jugs and smashes them into the recycling bin. He can get away with this. If I touch something out there, Ron will practically scream. *I still need that.* Ron has a deep affinity for anything plastic; he saves it all. He is a plastic junkie. But Tom has some sort of license. He spends two hours trimming the hedges and cleaning the gutters until he can't move his arms.

Today, Bunny doesn't know me. She asks Ron if I am his daughter. We agree that I am. What do I feel? I feel nothing. Or else, what I feel, I have placed in a drawer for later. I will grieve all of this when she is truly gone, not just mostly gone. My grief efficiencies have grown high; my years touring Dementia have altered me. I am bendy now, like a straw. If my mother doesn't know me today, she will know me next visit. I lower standards as fast as I can. Love is agility, I see now.

I go to my mother's bedroom and tackle her accessories and jewelry boxes. She has dozens of necklaces hanging on wooden mug racks. Several boxes filled with costume jewelry. Bunny has no need for accessories, shoes, or clothing. She is like Jesus that way. We have a small woven bowl with a few items that we give her again and again. Each time we give it to her is the first time. I place everything else into a giant bag and sled out like the Grinch.

On the way home, we stop at 1/4 Pound Giant Burgers and get cheeseburgers and root beer floats. What are we celebrating? Being alive. Being able bodied. Being—although this seems counterintuitive—young.

When I get the big bag of accessories home, I sort through it. Purses and hats galore. I throw some things away but then find myself dumping the garbage can out in the driveway to find the pair to an earring. Bunny never pierced her ears, and they are all clip-on. I like clip-ons because my ear holes are stretched out, and I look like a Maasai Ubangi tribe member. I think I am done and realize I am missing another earring. The garbage gets dumped out again. This time, I find the real treasure: a ring with tiny diamonds in it that she used to wear. Her small child's bracelet with a heart in the center; I remember playing with this as a child. It makes me happy to see it again. I can still play with it. I find the Mardi Gras beads I brought back to her from New Orleans. I find a locket with baby Pablo's picture in it. I find a glow-in-the-dark T-rex that is actually a whistle, which she placed on a cord for Pablo. I blow the whistle. It's good. A signal to the past and to the future, I imagine, to the place where all babies are in line to be born. Am I summoning a grandchild? I may be. I blow it again.

Magic Broth

In general, my mother didn't trouble herself with cooking, but she loved Thanksgiving, and her stuffing and gravy were flawless, never shunned by children. *The secret,* she always said, *is in the broth.* This she made on the day before Thanksgiving, from the turkey neck and giblets, the throwaway parts. What I think of as the magic broth.

The magic broth is used in the stuffing, in place of what my mother called the *bullshit canned broth.* It will also be used in the gravy instead of water or milk or stock. Wherever liquid is called for, we use the magic broth.

Here's how it's made.

Place the giblets and the neck of the bird into a big pot and cover it with water, three to four inches above the giblets. Add one large chopped onion, three cloves garlic, and four or five chicken bouillon cubes plus fresh ground pepper, and more salt if you like, but I never do. Simmer very low for five to eight hours, covered. You can do this as you sleep. I've done that.

Drain the broth through a fine sieve. Gather all the meat that's fallen off. Chop it fine and set it aside for the stuffing. When the broth has cooled, skim the fat off and refrigerate for the stuffing and gravy that you make the next day.

Every year, I bring my mother all these things. She who made magic out of throwaway parts so that we kids could steal away with precious Tupperware containers of juicy white meat and ambrosial gravy. I bring the art back to Michelangelo.

How To Surf

I'm not the same person after I entered this country as when I began, and neither is anyone else, I suspect. At the start, you're stretched thin and gasping for oxygen like Tom Hanks *in Apollo 13*, like Mike Teavee in *Willy Wonka* after being put through the taffy puller. You enter the country, and it's wily—you're in darkness; you're in Vietnam: the jungle rises to greet you. It can be lush with insight in the lack of pretense and prettification or dank with dread like a snake-infested swamp. You wade in and tack against the tide of death and degeneration. It whips you about, and if you can stand it, after a time you begin to surf, you begin to ride the waves of deliverance that are coming for your loved one, and the travel changes your form. You go all around to Heaven and Hell and back again, sometimes in the same day, the same hour. You are heavy with despair, yet you are also light somehow, light as the spirit your mother has become, a whispering thing, her spirit loosed, about to fly. Hanging on but barely, by a fine thread, by a pulse. She's given up her body, her limbs, her intellect, her ego. She's free now, on the cusp, and you've gotten to see it, the whole thing. The process of flight. Now you run alongside her, lifting her with your mind and your being, as she is a slim kite headed upward. Now you know how. Now you know what she knows. She's teaching you to her last breath. And beyond that? Her voice in your head, her essence that she deposited day by day, the wisdom she breathed into you. The kiss not of death, as you suspected, but the kiss of life. It has come full circle. She ushered you in; you're ushering her out. Grace is all. Roundness is all, this single revolution. And you know how it's going to end now. You can see it, like the end of a good book, like the end of a fine film, one that seemed dark but isn't. This is the finale you didn't see coming, the grand payoff. This is the happy ending you didn't expect; this is grace; this is the Director's cut. The master's cut. The final frame. You thought it would be ugly, but it isn't. It's beautiful.

The Waiting Place

I saved a box of Pablo's favorite baby books. I unpack them now. They feel holy.

A book falls; I pick it up. *Oh, The Places You'll Go!* It falls to a page we both really loved, The Waiting Place.

> *Everybody's just waiting. Waiting for the pot to boil or*
> *the mail to come or the phone to ring or the rain to go*

I think about everything I didn't know then. How when my first husband read this very book aloud with his wildly funny voices that *Oh!* one of the places he would soon go was to a family law office.

I think about my mother.

I think about my life before Tom. How it seems like a dream to me now.

I hear a ping. An MP3 arrives in my email. In it, my son plays something beautiful on his guitar. It sounds like rain falling on flat stones in an alley in Spain.

I take a breath. The world changes again.

Café Bustelo

At my mother's house, I boil the milk until it is just on the verge. Separately, I boil the water. I add the Café Bustelo instant powder because frankly this powder is as good as anything you might get in Milan or Paris. I wait until the brown water looks like thick mud and small bubbles appear. I pour in the milk, which has a skin now. I lift the bowl to my lips. I taste the caramel flavor of the whole milk I use, never low fat, not even if I am dying of morbid obesity and am down to my last dime.

Home, I think.

I am a Café Bustelo person. I am, in the final analysis, Boricua like my mother and Abuelita and so forth, all the way back to the very first Taino who looked around for a coconut shell to drink from.

Growing up, my mother said, *Don't give your power away*. It was more or less her first lesson. She had to save all of hers to sail to New York on the steamship Boriquen, away from Leonor. Saved it to survive mother loss and the diseases she carried from Mayaguez, saved it in order to dance with a tambourine, in a ruffled midriff top and skirt and tap shoes, face lit with joy.

But I did give it away. In handfuls, constantly. To my husband, yes, but also to people I feared and admired and people I wanted to like me. I had the demeanor of someone who wouldn't, but I did.

Now I don't. I need all my power for myself in order to regenerate, to grow back a mother within myself, to grow back a life without her.

And I don't need a reason why. This is a tremendous truth that I found at the bottom of the well.

The Tree Woman

There are pomegranates in our tree. Their tough skins look like mottled rubies, but inside there are live seeds. Delicious and crimson and full of juice. It's raining, and the sun is out: *Witches are getting married.* The weather echoes my mood. Two things at once, dark and light.

From my room I see the fog roll in and out, a soft white blanket of ease. I see the camellia tree and inside of it, what I've come to think of as the Japanese Tree Woman, made of wood, her long branch arms outstretched as she climbs out of her situation inside the Camellia japonica, which is an evergreen and never dies. Her breasts are low; her head is almost hollow. Everyday she climbs, presenting a graceful Sisyphus. This tree is a living telegram to me. Its glossy leaves curl skyward.

The tree woman, I imagine, will someday be totally free. She'll be reborn whole and walk into the woods and choose, perhaps, a new home.

She is my mother. She is me. She is everyone.

Dignity

There is dignity in Dementia as long as we say there is.

There is wisdom and humor and light, as long as we can see it.

I make the effort because my mother does and because it is what she deserves after a long life well lived, harming no one.

I am dazzled by her courage, even now. Especially now.

Nadine says that my mother is making me stronger, through endurance, as I bear witness to the end of her life.

I think she is handing over her strength, piece by piece, to me. The gift of a lifetime.

There's a song I listen to when I run that makes me surge even when I am tired called "We Found Love." It has a crazy disco beat, and Rihanna, and how love can be found in a hopeless place. At its bridge, a sound like supersonic rockets creates a mad, joyous crescendo. When I hear it, I think of my mother and what I want us to be, what we will never in this life be again. She will never stand by my side with her body and with her mind. But it doesn't matter. She's going up. I will meet her there.

Breakthrough

It's almost midwinter. Soon the light will begin to grow again. I'm watching the cedar waxwings tear the red berries off our tree when I see this on my Instagram: A picture of a mother and daughter.

ALZHEIMER'S DRUG LECANEMAB MAKES MOMENTOUS BREAKTHROUGH

@alzheimersresearchuk

"This announcement is very welcome news for families like ours."

Emily's mum, Janet was diagnosed with young-onset Alzheimer's disease in 2010, aged 60.

"We know this is too late for my mum as she is now very, very ill, with advanced Alzheimer's disease but throughout our journey, a comfort for us has been the hope that new treatments

will be found so in the future other families
won't have to go through the same experience."

It's only for new patients and it has some risks, but still.
This is the first time a drug has been shown to both reduce the
disease in the brain and slow memory decline in clinical trials.
Lecanemab was found inside a mouse antibody.

I smile.

Jesus has been watching all along and finally got sick of the
many calls and letters.

I watch the band of waxwings merrily rob the tree with
their black bandit masks, an insouciant frill of hair on the
crown. Their lime green chests thrust forth as they stuff the
red berries in their mouths and toss their head as if to say *Try to
catch us. We are life itself.*

Nature has a cure for everything, they counsel. *Things change.*

And then, by way of instruction and heeding a signal I can't
see, they all fly away.

Draw In the Stars

I walked around for sixty-four years with a protective casing of
love and magic. I feel its loss every day.

Now it's left to me to mourn, and then draw in the stars
myself. To navigate without my mother.

I see now that this isn't a story about my mother's descent.
It's the story of our family that she said I would write. It is her
final prediction, blooming like a hibiscus in Guayama, the city
of witches on the island of Puerto Rico. Blooming in the very
heart of Dementia.

EPILOGUE

There should be a crisp trajectory and a timely ending to this story, but there isn't. It's not that kind of opera, with three clear acts and a resounding finale. The actors—Ron, myself, Tom, my Greek Chorus—will not bow at the end; there will be no applause. We will shuffle off to our next life: the one without her. I will live without a mother as I have been living without a mother. Ron will live without a wife as he has been living without a wife. None of this is remarkable, and yet I feel a need to say, *We are down one Bunny. Send another baby girl to Mayaguez. Do it right away.*

ACKNOWLEDGMENTS

Nothing happens without the assistance of my agent Kimberly Witherspoon and Maria Whelan at Inkwell Management. I give thanks for the blithe comrades who helped me navigate the wilds of Dementia: Augusten Burroughs, Dee Alexich, Ken Woodard, William Dameron, and Carrie Wilson Link. Where would I be without my therapists Lyn Prashant and Claudia Sieber? The great Christopher Schelling provided early feedback that stopped me from harming myself. I am indebted to Abigail Thomas for her keen eye and editing prowess, and for showing me what memoir could be. Appreciation is owed to Debra Englander and Post Hill Press for their fine stewardship. I honor my Boricua family who have made me who I am. As always, my son, Pablo Finnamore Friedman, gives me levity and words to help light the darkness. My husband Tom Luckenbach is the rock upon which I stand. As always, I laud my mother Bunny, the strongest woman I have ever known. I bow low to my intrepid and kind stepfather Ronald Mathews, Bunny's primary caretaker.

Finally, I acknowledge and thank all caretakers and hospice workers, paid and unpaid, who are truly doing God's work.